**Houghton
Mifflin
Company**

Boston

*New York
Atlanta
Geneva, Illinois
Dallas
Palo Alto*

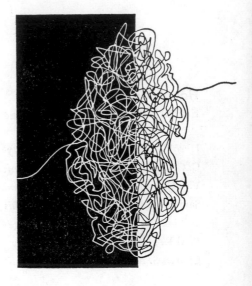

Intergroup

Relations

Charlotte Epstein
Temple University

for the

Classroom

Teacher

To my father

Foreword

In our times, the long hot summers of civil disorder and the long cold winters of racial unrest deeply trouble thoughtful Americans. The residents of a United States of America which is not sufficiently united teeter on the brink of separatism. Today we are reaping the bitter harvest of a social problem with roots deep in the American past.

Issues in human relations have become inescapable. Dealing with intergroup relations through American schools today is no longer a matter of teaching preference. Instead, the achievement of better human relations through education is an imperative necessity which is vital to national welfare and to the development of individual human beings.

To help the classroom teacher deal with intergroup relations is the purpose of this book by Charlotte Epstein. The author forthrightly supports desegregation with integration rather than segregation with separation as desirable national and classroom policies. In order to help in the betterment of intercultural relations, Dr. Epstein provides a guide to teachers who must inevitably encounter problems of human relations in their classrooms, whatever the social or racial or religious composition of the class members.

Many types of classrooms and students exist in American schools. Therefore, in the early chapters the author deals with the variety of settings in which teaching takes place. These include the one-group classroom, the multi-group classroom which is desegregated, and the multi-group classroom which is integrated. She takes up the problems of the various types of young people in these classrooms: middle-class majority children, middle-class minority children, poor majority children, poor minority children and suburban children. Throughout the chapters, she intersperses a variety of suggested techniques and approaches. Additional chapters identify intergroup problems in these varied settings and suggest possible solutions. As a realist who talks directly to teachers, the author takes up classroom discipline, the treatment of controversial subjects, and the relation of intergroup problems to school achievement.

Dr. Epstein recognizes that much instruction in American schools focuses upon the usual content of required subject matter. Therefore, in the closing chapters, she illustrates how such content may be utilized for better intergroup relations, whether the subject matter happens to be a Shakespearean play, the colonial period in history, arithmetic, or science.

The tone of the book is direct and forthright, unpretentious and honest. It should appeal to both the social vision and the common sense of the classroom teacher to whom the book is directed.

William Van Til
Coffman Distinguished Professor in Education
Indiana State University

Preface

Children are leaving our schools these days often unaware of the essential nature of the struggle that characterizes
our twentieth-century world. The reason for this vary: often
teachers are themselves uninvolved in the dynamics of struggle
and change. They just do not know the meaning of the turmoil, nor do they understand the feelings of the people who
are involved. Often, too, teachers are worried about the effects
on children of discussing events charged with conflicting emotions. More than anything, I think, teachers and other adults
are reluctant to face squarely what is happening in the world,
and to examine it honestly and openly. Such open examination is uncomfortable, because in the process we must come to
grips with our own preconceptions. We must also, especially
in the classroom, face open resistance to our own beliefs.

There is no quick and easy way to overcome the difficulty
of dealing with new and emotional subjects in the classroom.
Only continued practice in honest investigation and discussion will remove the discomfort.

However, this book is designed to make the process somewhat easier. The teacher is emphatically not being com-
manded to discard all the traditional subject matter and
familiar textbooks on which she has come to depend. The suggestion is, rather, that the traditional content be looked at in
the light of new data, contemporary events, and the feelings
and ideas of people who are living today. Some of those events,
feelings and ideas are first discussed in the book and then
related to some of the subjects taught in the schools. Teachers
may see from the examples how classroom activity may be
made more relevant to the students' lives.

But the most telling part of the book, I think, is the opening section of sixteen anecdotes which illustrates so tragically how much we have yet to learn. For help in the learning, we must look to those for whom this book is written. You are, after all, the ones who have volunteered to teach us.

Charlotte Epstein

Contents

Foreword **vii**

Preface **ix**

I

❛❛We don't have time for everything❜❜

Contamination : Age 3 **3**

Self-Rejection : Age 5 **4**

Black/White Dichotomization : Age 6 **5**

Overgeneralization : Age 7 **6**

Fear : Age 8 **7**

Denigration : Age 9 **8**

Alienation : Age 10 **9**

Isolation : Age 11 **10**

Self-Devaluation : Age 12 **11**

Stereotyping : Age 13 **12**

Separation : Age 14 **13**

Despair : Age 15 **15**

Destruction : Age 17 **16**

Exclusion : Engineer **17**

Brutalization : Bartender and Sheriff **18**

Suppression : Teacher **20**

II

"We have no intergroup problems"

1 / The One-Group Classroom   **23**

The Need for Intergroup Education
Hidden Needs for Intergroup Education
Causes of One-Group Schools
Causes of One-Group Classrooms
Educational Practices and Intergroup Relations

2 / The Multi-Group Classroom—
Desegregation   **32**

The Desegregated Situation
Desegregation and Communication
Tokenism
Bussing
Desegregation and Conflict

3 / The Multi-Group Classroom—Integration   **40**

Integration Defined
Needs and Methods

4 / The Teacher   **47**

Teachers' Special Skills
Intergroup Skills

III

"These are our problems"

5 / Intergroup Problems of Middle-Class
Majority Children   **57**

Isolation
Stereotyping
Delusion
White Power

6 / Intergroup Problems of Middle-Class
Minority Children   **64**

Differential Problems of White and Colored Minorities
Prejudice and Non-Participation
Intra-Group Prejudice

7 / Intergroup Problems of Poor Majority Children 70

Minority-Group WASPS
Poor Non-Spanish-Speaking Whites
Social Class Integration
Universal Needs in Intergroup Relations

8 / Intergroup Problems of Suburban Children 76

Working-Class Suburbs
Middle-Class Suburbs
Minorities in the Suburbs

9 / Intergroup Problems of Poor Minority Children 83

White Values
School Environment
Curriculum Factors
Unappreciated Strengths
Lack of Communication

10 / Identifying Intergroup Problems in the Classroom 91

Raising Issues
Encouraging Discussion
Observing Behavior
Sociometry
Analyzing the Fights
Recognizing Feelings
An Evaluation Checklist

11 / Solving Intergroup Problems in the Classroom 106

Taking the Initiative
Role-Playing
Cooperative Teaching
Exploding the Myth of Homogeneity
Seeing Discipline Problems as Internal Disharmony
Disseminating Facts

12 / Classroom Discipline and Controversial Subjects 116

Good Noise
Rule-Book Etiquette
Emotional Expression
Developmental Levels of Behavior
Self-Control
Discipline and Intergroup Relations

13 / The Relation of Intergroup Relations Problems to School Achievement   123

Self Concept
Effects of Desegregation on Achievement

IV

"We must cover the course of study"

Introduction   133

14 / Shakespeare's *Julius Caesar*—Teaching Intergroup Relations with a Traditional Text   135

Crowd Behavior
The Effect of Fear and Guilt on Judgment
Lack of Knowledge and Prejudgment
Dichotomous Thinking
Believing the People We Love
Attitudes Toward Authority
Inner Conflict and Hostility
Fear and Hostility
Unconscious Motivation in Human Behavior
Rationalization
Self-Hatred
Anger and Hostility
Ceremonials and Testimonials
Effecting Social Change
Methods of Teaching Intergroup Relations with *Julius Caesar*

15 / United States History—The Colonial Period   152

An Explanatory Note
Interreligious Relations
Intergroup Relations and Crime
Minorities and the Law
Minority Groups and American Civilization
Slavery in America
Inter-Class Relations
Human Relations and War
Americans in Rebellion

16 / Elementary Science—Food Preservation   167

An Explanatory Note
Hunger Then and Now

Refrigeration and Installment Buying
Poverty and Food Quality
Intergroup Relations and Food
Science and Cooperation

17 / Spelling—Contractions and Possessives   **173**

An Explanatory Note
Words and Meanings
Words and Attitudes
Language and Intergroup Relations

18 / Arithmetic—Seventh Grade   **178**

Arithmetic Problems and Life Problems
Interrelationship of Areas of Knowledge
Intergroup Relations by Analogy

19 / High School Biology—The Digestive System   **182**

An Explanatory Note
The Digestive System

20 / Anthologies for Children   **188**

Secondary Poetry and Prose
Elementary Readers

V

"Let's add it to the course of study"

Introduction   **197**

21 / Starting a Unit in Intergroup Relations— First Grade   **199**

An Explanatory Note
Goal and Purposes
The Initial Experience
Identifying with the Characters
Setting the Scene for Role-Playing
Observing the Interaction
Changing the Pattern of Interaction
Broadening the Scope of the Experience
Adding Experiences

Suggested Readings   **205**

Index   **211**

**Intergroup
Relations
for the
Classroom
Teacher**

I   **"We don't have time for everything"**

Teachers have never been able to transmit to children everything in the culture. They have always been faced with the necessity for making choices in order to devise a workable curriculum. That the choices have often been wise is evidenced in our strong and dynamic society. That we have sometimes made errors of omission is evident in the number of age-old problems our society has been unable to solve.

As the body of human knowledge grows and the complexities of human interaction proliferate, our choices become more critical. We are compelled to select from the vast store of our cultural panorama those concerns upon which our survival depends. We must continually refer back to the essential question, "What is man?" and make our curriculum choices on the basis of the answer.

At the very core of the nature of man is his interdependence. It is inconceivable that we could exist as isolate entities, with no will or ability to reach out to each other and touch. It is a fact, however, that our touch often maims and kills. What can we teachers do to make that reaching-out a more human thing? How can we preserve in ourselves and in our pupils the small child's capacity for oceanic response, a feeling of oneness with all humankind? How can all of us, in our everyday interactions, become more aware of each other's needs and pains?

We human beings begin very early to show our insensitivity to each other. Tiny children, innocent and malleable, wound themselves and others. Every year of their lives prejudice becomes more firmly fixed in their personalities. Each new experience is approached with the distorted perceptions and hostile expectations that past experiences have reinforced.

To say, as many people do, that children are free of prejudice and hostility is just not true. The anecdotes which follow are examples of things that happen all around us. The fearful, rejecting child becomes the fearful, rejecting adult. The men and women in our society who vote against open occupancy in housing, who refuse to consider some racial groups for high-level jobs, who see nothing wrong with keeping non-whites out of public facilities were once the three-year-olds and seven-year-olds and eleven-year-olds in these stories. This sickness does not suddenly attack grown people; the germ is transmitted very early in childhood. And the symptoms of the disease are evident in the behavior of people of all ages.

Each incident here reveals at least one behavioral symptom of the prejudice that lies at the core of our intergroup problems. But these incidents do not tell the whole story. Even the book does not do that. The whole story is part of the life of every citizen in a society where some are oppressed, some are oppressors, and most seem to be unaware of what is happening.

Contamination: Age 3

We sat in the living room, two friendly neighbors, resting for a moment from the chores of running a home and caring for children. Our two youngest children, both three years old, played quietly about the house. If asked, we would have said that our children had been reared without prejudice. In a world of war and discrimination, hostility and prejudice, our children were happy, friendly and accepting. At the very least, they knew nothing about differences in skin color and race and cared less.

As we sat, silent for a moment, we heard the two children chatting. Their voices seemed to come from behind the sofa on which we were sitting. Slowly, we became aware of what the little voices were saying:

"Are you scared?" my Barbara asked.

"I'm scared," said Kathy, and her three-year-old voice deepened and trembled. "I'm scared of colored."

Silence.

Kathy's voice whispered, "Colored are bad."

And Barbara's indignant voice: "I don't want you to tell me that! My mother doesn't tell me things like that!"

Self-Rejection: Age 5

The kindergarten teacher leaned against the wall and closed her eyes. The children were all busy with their crayons. She had given them each a mirror and asked them to draw their own faces, and they seemed intrigued by the idea. After a moment, she began to walk among the children, watching, encouraging and offering an occasional suggestion.

She stopped at the desk of a very quiet little boy, who often sat big-eyed, watching everything going on around him, forgetting the book in his lap or missing his turn in a game. Now she watched him staring into the small mirror in his hand, while the outline of a face remained unfinished on the paper in front of him. Then he turned from the mirror, his small brown face stiff with determination, and picked a black crayon from the box. He scribbled the outlined face, blacker and blacker, digging the crayon again and again into the paper until it tore. Then he carefully crumpled the paper into a wad, took it to the waste basket and dropped it in.

Black/White Dichotomization: Age 6

Billy was having trouble with his teacher. He was sure she didn't like him, and he knew *why* she didn't like him, too. He just couldn't seem to please her, no matter what he did. She was always at him: "Stop this. Don't do that. Stand outside. Go back to your seat." He just didn't like school any more on account of that old teacher.

Once again, he found himself on the detention bench outside the principal's office. He could feel the tears well up in his eyes and roll down his face as he waited for Mr. Riley to notice him.

And then Mr. Riley was looming over him, stern-faced but with a twinkle in his eye. "Well, Billy. I hear you are having a problem."

Billy did not trust himself to speak. He nodded his head as the tears kept rolling.

"Come into my office," said Mr. Riley, putting his arm around the boy, "and we'll see if we can straighten this out."

Seated, facing each other, man and boy felt a bond of affection and understanding. "I don't like Miss Colter," Billy half-cried, half-shouted.

"Oh? Tell me why."

"Because she's white!"

Mr. Riley was puzzled. "You like *me*, don't you? I thought you liked *me*."

For a minute, the tears stopped flowing. "Yes, I like *you*. But *you're* colored!"

Mr. Riley thought of the endless line of his red-haired Irish forbears stretching into the distant past and pondered the problem of this child who saw all his likes and dislikes in terms of white and colored.

Overgeneralization: Age 7

Several boys and girls were tossing a ball around and all running after it when one of them missed a catch. The woman walking up to one of the nearby houses stopped to watch and to listen to the sounds of laughter and excited screaming. It was a mild Spring day. In this quiet suburban community, the lawns were becoming green again and leaves were beginning to appear on the trees. The clumps of bright yellow forsythia were especially pleasing to the woman, who saw only the bricks and pavements of city streets for six days a week. It was good to have a sister to visit out here, good to smell the grass warmed by the sun, good to watch the children playing, her adored niece among them.

At dinner with her sister, brother-in-law and the seven-year-old niece, who had run in from her game to hug and kiss her aunt, the talk was casual and friendly. "I see real life has come to Winton," the visitor teased. To the child, she said, "I noticed you have a little Japanese friend."

"Yes. He's Jimmy. Tommy says Japs kill Americans."

Husband and wife looked at each other, startled.

"No, dear." the sister-in-law sounded a little breathless. "Jimmy is an American too. The war with Japan was over a long time ago."

"Oh." The child did not seem concerned. But her parents and her aunt were silent for a long time.

Fear: Age 8

Steven was eight years old today, and he was looking forward to his party this afternoon. He had accompanied his mother to the corner grocery store to buy the ingredients for a birthday cake. "With lots of icing on top," he had instructed her. Mr. Green, the grocer, had wished him a happy birthday and handed him a bunch of lollipops across the counter.

Now he squatted at the curb, watching the swirling river in the gutter through a pleasant mist of anticipation. Suddenly his reverie was broken, and he was afraid.

This face looming in front of him was no longer the face of the friendly grocer who gave him lollipops. The eyes bulged with menace, and Steven felt his breath come in quick, shallow gasps. The voice faded and then boomed loud again, ". . . ready . . . party?" He was frozen motionless and voiceless. This was the Jew. Johnny had told him about Jews . . . what *had* he told him? Johnny's father didn't like Jews . . .

The grocer nodded and smiled and walked on.

Denigration: Age 9

After all the children had been assigned to their seats, Connie raised her hand.

"Yes, Connie?" said Miss Danforth. "What is it?"

"May I speak to you, Miss Danforth?" The voice was full of portent and the tone asked for privacy.

"Yes, of course." Miss Danforth beckoned the child to her desk. "Now," she lowered her voice, "what's the trouble?"

Connie leaned closer. "My mother doesn't want me to sit in that seat," she confided.

Miss Danforth was puzzled. She hated the rows of double seats bolted to the floor. It left so little opportunity for flexible grouping and cooperative learning. But this was the first day of the new school year, and the children had hardly been in their seats five minutes. What *did* the child mean?

"Why not, Connie? What's the matter with the seat?"

"Well. . . . My mother says they're dirty and I'm not supposed to get too close to them."

Miss Danforth looked at Madrilena Lopez, who shared the double seat with Connie, and began to revise her plans for this year's teaching.

Alienation: Age 10

I think my school is nice because of the way it is run, in order and we stay at school for lunch. But, you can't move unless the chairs go with you. It's cheap because we have to buy our own paper every week or so. Why can't this school buy paper? We should have lockers and we should have soup on rainy days. There is no good Home and School Association, and we need more supplies for the school. The rooms still have same coat of paint since when the school was built. When a water fountain is out of order, it stays out of order for a month. If we had more mothers helping, we would have the supplies and the football and baseball games after school like other schools. I haven't been having any fun since I got to school. The busses are a sight. They should put somebody on the bus to watch the kids. Lucky I'm not catching the school bus any more. At Averson, Mr. Hoder was like a father to us kids. He knew how to understand our problem. I can't say no more but *cheap*.

Isolation: Age 11

Mr. Miller used a simple sociometric technique to identify the more isolated children in his class. "Whom would you choose to sit next to during the assembly program?" he had written on the chalk board. Some children were chosen again and again. Some were not chosen at all.

On another day, he administered the *Ohio Recognition Scale: Who's Who in My Group,* which asks such questions as: "Do we have any boys and girls in our room who are very even-tempered, who almost never get upset or angry, who are always calm when things go wrong? Who are they?"

"There are some children who are strong enough to win fights but they don't pick fights. They don't go around teasing and hitting people. They stop 'bullies' from hitting and teasing smaller children. They want everyone to have a square deal. Do we have any children like that? Who are they?"

When the time came for the children to work on their social studies project, Mr. Miller decided to put some of the more isolated children into groups with children who were viewed as warm, accepting and helpful.

Two days later he asked for informal reports on how the groups were progressing. One girl burst out crying. Mr. Miller took her outside for a drink of water and, when she had become calmer, asked her what was wrong.

"My team doesn't want me," she said. "They don't like me."

"How do you know, Janie? Did they say so?"

"No. I just know, that's all."

Janie was one of the isolated children. Janie was Negro. The other two children on her team were white. How much of Janie's isolation was due to her race?

Self-Devaluation: Age 12

Dear Mrs. Sutter:

I know I am not a good student and I am a problem to the class. Thank you for spending your time with me yesterday. But don't be wasteing your time with me. I am a nobody.

Carol

Stereotyping: Age 13

Donna listened to her mother and the visitor talking about the demonstration in favor of integrated schools. "We have two colored kids in our school this year," she said.

"You've never had Negro children in your school before?" asked the visitor.

"No. And these two boys—they're brothers—they're real great dancers. Colored kids are terrific dancers."

"You've seen these two boys dance?"

"No. But everyone knows colored kids can really dance. They're great."

Separation: Age 14

The city is in an uproar because a boy has been badly beaten and is in serious condition in the hospital. The beating occurred during a street fight between two groups of boys from the same school. The police say that there is no evidence the boys had been members of organized gangs. The fight apparently started over the right to use a dead-end street near the school for a ball game.

One group of boys lives near the disputed street and insists that they have sole right to use it. They have been playing ball there—off and on—for several years. It is one of these boys who is in the hospital.

The other boys do not live nearby. They are bussed to school each morning, and are ordinarily bussed home as soon as classes are over. But the day of the fight they had decided to walk home. On the way, they had come upon the small dead-end street and stopped to throw a ball around. The neighborhood boys appeared, and an argument began.

The neighborhood people are insisting that the incident is an inevitable result of bussing children to the school from another part of the city. The bussed-in children are troublemakers, they say, and no good can ever come of this practice. They had always been against bussing, and now they feel their stand has been vindicated.

The principal of the school insists that what has happened is not the fault of the school. It is impossible, he says, to force the boys to get on the bus after school each day, though every effort would be made to insure that they did so from now on. He has confided privately to his vice-principal that he hopes the injured boy recovers quickly so that the matter may blow over, because this kind of turmoil is detrimental to learning.

The Commission on Human Relations maintains that, though the neighborhood boys are white and the bussed-in boys are Negro, the incident was just a fight between two groups of kids, and certainly did not indicate interracial tension.

The school is situated in a neighborhood settled three generations ago by immigrants from Ireland, and two generations ago by people from Italy. Some of the inhabitants have distant memories of conflict between the Irish and the Italians, but they insist that there is no antagonism between the groups now. They point to examples of intermarriage in this generation and laugh at the horrified reactions of some of the grandparents to such marriages.

In the past few years a number of Negro families have moved to a street near the neighborhood. These families are strictly ignored by the older residents surrounding them. In the school, the children of these families have apparently been absorbed into the regular program without incident or comment.

Most of the people in the neighborhood are upper lower-class—predominantly workers in the building trades, with some police officers and some owners of small businesses like hoagie shops and grocery stores.

The bussed-in children come from a school that had been on double session until this year. The school is fed from the immediate neighborhood, which is entirely Negro. Most of the people in the neighborhood work at unskilled jobs and many are periodically on relief. However, there are some who are police officers, sanitation department workers, post office employees and small business owners.

The principal has his wish: the incident eventually recedes into the past. But in the school, Negro and white students keep their distance from each other as they did before, race relations are never discussed and no Negro or white youngster feels comfortable in the vicinity of the school alone.

Despair: Age 15

The teacher had distributed papers with directions mimeographed on top: Write for 15 minutes on *How I Think About My School*.

And the child had written:

I think my school is black because only black go. The people in charge is nice, but some teacher's are not too good. They don't make the children be quiet, don't put there foot down and that just messes it up for everyone. It's a slum. This school is just not for me. I could never be proud of this school in this section. Well maybe in another section I could bring up my grades. I could be proud because I would have a lot to be proud of.

Destruction: Age 17

The crowd outside the Smiths' home grew louder. Laughter was giving way to jeering and catcalls and the sound was menacing. The size of the crowd had been growing since seven o'clock, when the moving van had pulled up to the house with the new family's belongings. Though there were a few adults in front of the house, the shouting and obscenities came mostly from youngsters—teenagers.

"Go back where you came from, niggers!"

"We don't want niggers in our neighborhood!"

The ten policemen who stood in a line in front of the house joked with the crowd. One boy in the front of the crowd held one of the policemen's night sticks in his hand and was swinging it playfully like a bat. Occasionally, a rock would fly over the heads of the policemen and hit the door or wall of the house.

The rock-throwing became more frequent, and the crowd began to push against the line of policemen.

Suddenly a shower of rocks hit the front of the house and glass shattered. A policeman lay spreadeagled on the ground, blood pouring from a gash on his forehead. In an upstairs window, the terrified face of a child appeared for a moment and jerked out of sight.

Exclusion: Engineer

The university professor and his wife were answering a house-for-sale advertisement. The look of surprise on the face of the woman who opened the door was lost on them.

"I am Dr. Chen. This is my wife. We're interested in buying a house in this area, and we saw your ad."

"Well . . . uh . . . My- my husband isn't home."

"If we could just look at the house? Then, if it's suitable, we could come back another time and talk to your husband."

"Uh . . . I don't know . . . I don't think my husband . . .". The woman stuttered, and her embarrassment became increasingly apparent. At the sound of footsteps coming up the walk, she looked visibly relieved. "Here's my husband now," she said quickly, turning back into the house and shutting the door behind her.

The Chens looked at each other and at the man coming toward them.

"Yes?" he said briskly when he was more than ten feet from them. "What is it?"

Dr. Chen introduced himself again and began to explain.

"No, no," the man interrupted. "The house is not for sale. The house is not for sale." And then he, too, disappeared behind the slammed door.

The advertisement appeared in the newspaper for two more weeks before it was discontinued. Several days after that, the new owners' name appeared on the mailbox: *The Carltons*.

Brutalization: Bartender and Sheriff

A young Indian couple enter the local tavern. It is early Saturday night, and the regular tavern customers have not yet begun to trickle in for the weekend merrymaking. One or two men sit on stools, elbows on the bar, just as they have sat since early afternoon. The woman owner of the bar stares at the Indian couple and then moves her foot to an alarm signal under the bar.

The young man seats the young woman at one of the small tables and approaches the bar. "Two beers, please," he says.

"We don't serve Indians here."

The young woman gets up and moves to the man's side. "Why not?" she asks. "Don't we have a right?" She leans forward in indignation. The woman behind the bar shoves her brutally, and she falls to her knees.

Suddenly the sheriff appears, in answer to the alarm signal that had flashed in his office. He is carrying his gun. Without stopping to ask any questions, he rushes at the Indian man and begins to beat him with the gun. The young woman rushes to her friend's aid and is thrown back violently, with a cut down the side of her face.

Several men, some Indian and some white, see the fight through the plate glass window and rush in to join it. A deputy sheriff also appears, swinging a blackjack. The fight spills out into the street.

By evening, ten Indian men and two Indian women are in jail. No whites have been arrested. When the sheriff is interviewed, he is asked why he began to hit the Indian before asking any questions or learning what had happened. He assures the interviewer that, "These Indians are troublemakers. There's only one language they understand, and by damn, I speak it. I'm gonna teach them to act civilized or stay where they belong."

For weeks after the incident, the statistics of the town clearly confirm the allegation that Indians commit more crimes than whites.

Suppression: Teacher

Miss Jones found herself in a seminar on problems of interracial relations in the schools. The other members of the seminar were teachers and principals studying for the doctorate. Miss Jones was relieved that, at least, there were no Negroes in the group. But she still felt uncomfortable. She just didn't like to talk about such things.

The seminar leader listened closely to the discussion:

"I don't think you ought to talk about race relations unless the children bring it up. If they have a question, they'll ask."

"But children learn very quickly that there are some things they're not supposed to talk about. They won't ask questions about race—not when they're nine and ten years old."

"Well, there are no uh-uh . . . We have no problems in our school. I mean, all the children are uh . . . the same."

"No problems! You've got problems! Your children will have to meet and work with Negro people all their lives. How will they do it? They've *really* got problems."

"We have a uh . . . uh . . . a teacher who is uh . . . uh . . ."

Suddenly the leader realized what was happening. *Miss Jones could not say the word 'Negro'!*

II “We have no intergroup problems”

1 The One-Group Classroom

The Need for Intergroup Education

There are not many writers on intergroup relations today discussing the one-group school or one-group classroom with an eye to the need of the students for intergroup relations education. The belief is prevalent that the best education requires an integrated setting, in which children of different groups learn to live and work with each other and to accept each other as equally valuable human beings. I do not deviate one iota from this position: *there is no optimum education without integrated education.* However, the inescapable fact is that our schools generally are not being desegregated, while integration is not even seen as a realistic goal. (See Chapters 3 and 4 for a discussion of the difference between desegregation and integration.) For years many children will continue to be educated in one-group schools and one-group classrooms. While some of us work frantically to change this situation, all of us must do whatever is possible to reduce the harmful effects of segregated schools.

First, of course, it is necessary to realize that there *are* harmful effects. Apparent harmony does not always indicate real harmony. The person who is quiet, and even docile, may be seething with unexpressed emotions which can be more harmful than if they were expressed. Unexpressed strong feelings can destroy creativity, and can even make people physically ill. Undeniably, the energy used to disguise them, and keep them from spilling over, can be used more productively. And such feelings have a tendency to burst out unexpectedly and violently at an innocent object, in complete disproportion to the immediate stimulus. Thus, a police officer with strong negative feelings toward Indians may severely beat an Indian suspect who does nothing more than pull away from him. Perhaps the violence of his own response will startle and even frighten him—just before he rationalizes it away. One ranking police officer spoke articulately about the right of civil rights advocates to demonstrate, but his real feelings became apparent when, during a demonstration, he seized a picketer by the collar and almost strangled him before he was pulled away by fellow officers.

The unrealistic self-image that can result from segregated schools is reflected not only in school achievement, but also in the achievements and relationships of a lifetime. The Puerto Rican child who is convinced by a lifetime of segregation that he cannot compete with whites, will not apply for a college or job where such competition is necessary. Or, forced into a competitive situation, he will be unable to succeed because of his certainty of failure. The majority child, convinced that there is something inherently superior in his whiteness, becomes confused and angry if, as an adult, he finds himself in a situation in which race is no criterion for worth.

Many teachers, administrators and other adults interested in the schools believe that if a classroom is made up exclusively of children belonging to one group, there can be no intergroup problems. This belief has become a rationale for resisting the introduction of curriculum materials which deal with interracial, interethnic or interreligious relations. "We have no problems here," is the conclusion many draw from the apparent harmony of the one-group classroom. If disharmonies do become apparent, they are invariably attributed to factors that have no relevance to intergroup difficulties.

Certainly, there is no reason for the teacher of an all-Negro class to think that a fight between two of her pupils has any *intergroup* ramifications! Or is there? Has she ever heard one Negro child call another "nigger"? Surely this is an epithet one would expect only a white child to use. But why would one Negro call another such a name? First, let us examine what the word means. All racial, nationality and religious epithets —gook, wop, greaser, pape, kike—have the same disparaging implications for all groups. In general, these epithets imply that the individuals in a group are all alike, that the group is inferior to the speaker's own group, that the group is menacing in some way and that the group's traits are inborn. Such epithets also imply specific beliefs about each group: Negroes are oversexed, Orientals are sly, Ladinos are lazy, Catholics conspire to control, Jews cheat, and so forth.

When a Mexican child calls another "greaser" or a Jewish child uses the word "kike," why are we so quick to conclude that he means something different by it? The problem for the minority child may very well be compounded, for he is saying, in effect, "your minority groupness makes you inferior and *so does mine!*" Such an attitude is much more difficult to live with than a feeling of rejection toward another group. Perhaps we must conclude that it is *American* children who learn these words, and all that they imply, and that it is all American children—Indian or white, Negro or Oriental—who need help in changing their intergroup feelings and perceptions.

One of the most important reasons for teaching intergroup relations in the one-group classroom is to help the minority child cope with his immediate, personal experience of prejudice and discrimination. He lives in a world in which he is bound to have such experiences, and he almost invariably needs help in handling them. He needs to learn to show the prejudiced person that he is not only wrong, but that he cannot discriminate against people with impunity. The minority child must also be helped to emerge from the experience with his self-respect and self-confidence unimpaired. And all this must be done—if we are to adhere to our middle-class ethic—without physical violence! There is a formidable job of teaching required here, and an equally formidable job of learning for the minority child. For the minority child must, in spite of the prejudice of the majority, continue to *know* that he is not inferior.

Hidden Needs for Intergroup Education

Teachers of one-group classes often say with sincerity that they do not think their students even think about race problems. Parents will say this too, sometimes in an effort to demonstrate how free from intergroup conflict their children are. One Negro parent described her attitude toward intergroup education by suggesting that it was like sex education—if children came to you with questions, you answered them. Otherwise, you did not bring up the subject.

In the one-group classroom, the children's inner feelings are likely to be obscured by emphasis on homogeneity, by avoidance of emotionally-toned knowledge and by insistence on external order. Pressure to conform often makes children reluctant to be the first to express an opinion, voice curiosity about an event or to put their feelings into words. We have all seen the classroom results of being "different." Often the other children laugh, in derision or embarrassment, at a child who expresses himself openly, and the teacher's usual response is a demand for "order." Sometimes, the teacher regards the "different" statement as interference with her educational aims or a distracting injection of extraneous material. She may discourage such interruptions by refusing to discuss the child's comment or by reprimanding him. In time, she may be able to delude herself into thinking that her children are not concerned with what is going on all around them, and particularly that they are uninterested in subjects like race and sex. It is possible that the subjects we exclude from the curriculum, and discourage children from discussing, are most likely to reveal elements of disharmony, confusion and conflict in and among the children.

Logic alone can help us see the irrationality of maintaining that the children in a class are free of intergroup tension just because they are all of the same ethnic group. How free from inner conflict can a child be when he is confronted daily with evidence that his society rejects him? Is it logical to suppose that inner conflict is not reflected in the behavior of the child? Restlessness, a high noise and confusion level and lack of interest in learning are pointed to repeatedly by teachers and laymen alike as evidence of the unteachability of poor children. It seems far more likely that such behavior results from lessons already learned, lessons that cause the inner turmoil we are prone to see as lack of discipline.

And what about the children whose unrealistic self-images are based on implications in the world around them that they are superior because they are members of one race rather than another? Sooner or later every child must face the necessity for reconciling democratic aphorisms with undemocratic behavior. What does this conflict do to children? How long is the period of confusion through which they must pass? What effect does the need to live with contradiction have on their personal integrity and self-respect? (Remember George Orwell's barnyard animal, who believed in equality but justified the undemocratic society by maintaining that some people are more equal than others!)

Perhaps the next time the children in our classes "correctly" answer the question, "What is a democracy?" we might venture a little bit beyond the accepted definition and examine the meaning of democracy in their everyday human relationships and in their not-so-deeply hidden feelings.

Causes of One-Group Schools

School people have often maintained that the one-group school, though it may not offer all the experiences children need, was not the invention of teachers or administrators and could not be changed by them. It is true, of course, that much of the segregation of groups in separate schools is a result of segregated housing patterns. But it is also undoubtedly a fact that school people have planned school sites, arranged school feeder patterns, and delineated school districts so as to provide for one-group schools. Teachers and principals, school boards and supervisors are products of our society just as are the other segments of the community. And most of us have contributed, in one way or another, to the pattern of segregation: some of us have actively supported separation, some have feared the effects of resistance, and others have merely felt powerless to change the pattern.

Sometimes segregation is maintained by such evasion and circumlocution, such patent lack of logic that the observer is dazed into speechlessness. Witness the president of a board of education who reaffirmed his board's stand that quality education means integrated education, and then proceeded in the same speech to justify his district's lack of progress toward integration by saying that the divergent opinions in the community must be reconciled. It would be interesting to know how much attention would be paid to reconciling divergent opinion on the value of teaching arithmetic in the schools!

At any rate, no matter what part we have played in perpetuating segregation, it is time to examine the whole problem of segregated schools and segregated classrooms in terms of our professional goals. For, though we recognize increasingly the importance of total community participation in the improvement of education, we are the education experts, it is we who know how children learn and we who must assume responsibility for the fact that most of them are not learning some very important lessons.

Causes of One-Group Classrooms

The school that serves more than one racial or ethnic group does not necessarily provide for intergroup experience. Schools have come to be called integrated when, in reality, they still offer segregated education for most of the school population.

Even when a school is desegregated (that is, populated by more than one racial or ethnic group) we are often almost inadvertently betrayed into continuing to maintain one-group classrooms. This is easily accomplished if we fall into the trap of using traditional educational methods in a situation which calls for ingenious innovation. This is the usual progression of events:

1. A community has a crowded all-Negro school and an underutilized all-white school.
2. The community decides to send Negro children to fill the vacant seats in the white school.
3. The Negro school has, for generations, been short of books and has had a higher proportion of substitute and inexperienced teachers.
4. Teachers in the Negro school have had low expectations for their Negro pupils. (Middle-class teachers have not expected much from lower-class children; white teachers have not expected much from Negro children.)
5. Low teacher expectations have led to indifferent teaching. Low pupil expectations have led to indifferent learning. Consequently, the Negro children have had a generally lower level of achievement.
6. Low-achieving Negro children are sent to the white school, where the children are grouped homogeneously on the basis of achievement.
7. Though some white low-achievers will end up in classes with Negro low-achievers, and Negro high-achievers will end up in classes with white high-achievers, most of the lowest achievers among Negro children will end up in all-Negro classes.

In addition, many teachers will persist in their low expectations of Negro and poor children, and the one-group class will be perpetuated in a desegregated school.

Another school desegregation technique used recently tends to reinforce the pattern of classroom segregation. In transferring minority children from an overcrowded school to an underutilized one, selection is made on the basis of the distribution of achievement levels in the receiving school. Because of the quality of education in most sending schools, a large proportion of the children are low-achievers. What happens, then, is that a disproportional percentage of the minority school's high-achievers are siphoned off, and the school is left with mostly low achievers. No majority children are, of course, sent to such a school, and the result is an all-minority school of extremely low-achieving children, who are caught forever in a cycle of low expectations. Furthermore, receiving schools are usually provided with maximum special services, like reading specialists and teacher aides, while the sending school continues to have inadequate facilities and personnel.

Nor does the desegregated school necessarily provide for out-of-class contact across ethnic lines. It has been observed that, even if children of different groups sit side by side in the classroom, they separate for lunch and for extra-curricular and out-of-school activities. If they are separated in classes, it is unlikely that they will voluntarily break the traditional pattern outside of class.

Educational Practices
and Intergroup Relations

As a profession we have expressed our commitment to the education of the whole child. This necessarily involves teaching the child to relate effectively to people who are different from himself. We have, as a profession, decried the conformist pressures which stifle originality and creativity. But the habit of conforming to racial and ethnic criteria in selecting our friends and associates is as stifling as life in Huxley's *Brave New World* of assembly-line people. As teachers, we have tried to understand children's needs and to provide for the satisfaction of those needs in the learning-developing situation. Yet hundreds of thousands of children leave school lacking in self-confidence, unaware of the complexity of the world they are entering, falsely confident or despairing. We teachers have contributed to the growth of a vital, dynamic society, filled with curious, creative people, who are often generous, often sensitive and often friendly. However, some of our citizens have never taken a significant part in the creative dynamism of our world. Even the means and methods we use in our schools have often had the effect of nullifying our stated professional goals. Our attempts to reach our goals have often, in effect, been antagonistic to those goals.

Specifically, we say we want to encourage individual development and yet we try to teach 30 or 35 children the same subject at the same rate. We want to teach acceptance of differences, yet we divide children into homogeneous groups. We want to foster curiosity and adventurous exploration in children, yet we encourage fear, hostility and avoidance when we accept the segregation that fosters misconceptions about other groups.

Sometimes the paradoxes built into the practice of our profession become so dramatically apparent to us that we must be, at least momentarily, horrified at what we are doing. I remember a young Indian girl who attended an all-white public school for most of her life. She grew up afraid of Indians, like the other children around her, and spent twenty years trying to overcome the effects of her education.

All this criticism may sound unnecessarily self-immolative. However, the burden of educational criticism must be taken from the public at large and placed where it belongs: with professional educators. If we do not begin to re-examine vigorously the principles and practices that characterize our profession, we will find ourselves led by vocal and efficiently organized political groups which seek to dictate what and how we teach. There are organizations that want American history to be presented as a series of supermoral decisions made by supermen: in their view, there must be no questioning or hint of criticism of American government past or present. There are organizations that advocate white teachers for white children and colored teachers for colored children. There are organizations that want the teaching of science adapted to their own religious beliefs. There are organizations that want us to revert to teaching only reading, writing and arithmetic. Some want only vocational education for all poor children;

others want to lower the school-leaving age. If we do not subject our means and goals to the cold light of logic and rationality, we will betray ourselves into the hands of those who would force us to abandon those goals.

History has left us a heritage of intergroup strife. The one-group school reinforces the divisions between groups and perpetuates barriers to understanding and acceptance. We need not live in guilt for what those before us have done or neglected to do. But we can accept the responsibility for doing what must be done in our own lifetimes.

2 The Multi-Group Classroom— Desegregation

The Desegregated Situation

Many of us who have suddenly become aware of the effects of segregation and the need for integration are overwhelmed by the magnitude of the job of changing the social pattern of isolation and rejection to one of optimal interaction. Some of us cope with this feeling of helplessness by suggesting that the job is done when children of different groups are brought together in the same school. Others are simply unaware of the developmental stages of feeling and behavior which precede true integration.

There is an essential difference between desegregation and integration, and the casual use of the two words as synonyms has led to the obfuscation of some important education issues. Let us first look at the desegregated school and the desegregated classroom. It is likely that we will recognize them as familiar situations which we have erroneously come to refer to as integrated.

There is a variety of circumstances in which majority- and minority-group children attend the same schools. In suburban areas, the number of minority children is usually negligible, partly due to employment discrimination, which has kept minority people poor, and partly because of the discriminatory housing practices which keep minority people in big-city ghettoes. Except for the few areas which have desegregated by consolidating their schools, there are not many suburban cases of meeting across race lines.

In urban areas, there is every kind of desegregated school. One type has a majority of children of the dominant local group and anywhere from two to two hundred children from a single minority group. Sometimes the minority children have been bussed into the school to relieve extreme overcrowding in their sending school. Sometimes these minority children make a point of voluntarily travelling long distances to a "good" school; they pay their own fares for the privilege of escaping from double sessions, old buildings, inadequate supplies and unprepared teachers. Sometimes the minority-group children live in the area of the school but are isolated in the neighborhood, psychologically if not physically. Occasionally, one or two minority children may move with their families into previously all-majority neighborhoods.

Whatever the pattern of desegregation, interaction within the school often reveals an actual separation of the majority and minority pupils. The children may pass each other in the corridors, sit side by side in classrooms and rarely engage in open conflict with each other. But they do not, in any real sense, recognize each other as sentient human beings. In rushing past each other they are aware, at most, of their own feelings only. At the least, they hardly recognize the other group's existence.

Desegregation and Communication

Desegregation, then, is the mere physical proximity of majority and minority children within the walls of a school building or a classroom. There may be only a handful of minority pupils among hundreds of majority children—or the reverse. But in a desegregated school, communication across group lines tends to be minimal or even entirely nonexistent. More significantly, no one recognizes this communications gulf as a problem or attempts to bridge it. One of the most destructive effects of confusing desegregation with integration is this belief that physical proximity alone is the ultimate goal in intergroup relations, and that it dispels the need to ask probing questions about what is really happening between groups. We have so much else to accomplish in our classes that it is a relief to assume that we need not concern ourselves with the nature of the communication across group lines, or devise ingenious opportunities for pupils to attempt meaningful communication with each other.

By "communication across group lines," we do not mean just the casual exchange of comments about a ball game or the English assignment. It is amazing how long people can brush by each other in this way without ever seeing each other very clearly. This kind of casual surface contact allows us to cover up real feelings, and we point to such apparently amiable contact as evidence that we have no prejudices. "I treat people the way they treat me," is the facile, complacent rationale for this kind of intergroup behavior. But should the nature of the contact change just a little, negative feelings immediately rush to the surface. If someone is accidentally pushed, it is "those people" who are "always" pushing; if an individual does not bathe often enough, it is "those people" who smell bad. Such apparently casual contact becomes almost an exercise in tight-rope-walking. The slightest mishap will cause the "no-problem" situation to disintegrate.

The teacher may be entirely unaware of the children's discomfort with each other. Feuds may go on between groups, hostile looks and quiet insults may be exchanged which the teacher never sees or hears. Certain children may be ignored outside of class, excluded from popular activities or isolated during lunch, and the teacher may never know about it. Seeing brown and white faces interspersed in an assembly, hearing responses from white and brown children in class, she may say in all honesty, "We have no intergroup problems here."

Just as children avoid talking about matters they feel strongly about for fear of losing control, causing overt conflict or confronting their own hostility and rage, so teachers avoid similar matters in the classroom for similar reasons. But, subtly or overtly, our hostilities find expression; and facing our fear of possible overt conflict is not as destructive as are the subtle wounds inflicted by unvoiced hatreds. Young people, like their mothers and fathers and teachers, have opinions, feelings and prejudices about other groups, and it is unrealistic to assume that these feelings and ideas do not influence their relationships with other groups.

Teachers are often unaware of a communication gap among students because of the enormous communication gulf between them and their students. This was impressed on me in a particularly painful way when the university in which I was teaching was considering taking a controversial step. The issue was widely discussed, but no factions had yet formed. Informally discussing the issue with a group of my students, they told me that if I decided to approve of the step, they would line up against me. When I asked why, they told me candidly that they would inevitably oppose whatever I supported because I was faculty and they were students. The intensity of the shock I felt was commensurate with my sincere belief, up to that point, that these students and I had developed excellent patterns of communication and that we understood each other very well.

It seems likely that the teacher of elementary and secondary students is faced with greater problems in communication than is the college teacher. For one thing, the age gap is greater with younger students. But probably even more significant is the traditional pattern of classroom communication: most of the talking is done by the teacher. When pupils talk, it is usually in response to a direct question from the teacher, who thus controls the pattern of communication in the classroom. It is axiomatic that when one person has authority, communication flows largely from the top down, and very little significant communication takes place in the other direction.

For the teacher who protests that, though she is firm in maintaining order, her pupils are free to talk about anything, we recall the police captain who prided himself on having optimal communication in his units. "My door is always open," he would boast. "My men know they can speak to me about anything." But, oddly, very few ever did. The captain didn't realize the numerous barriers to communication inherent in the very nature of the police organization. The psychological barrier against disagreeing with a superior officer, and the social barrier of traditional etiquette between ranks, was enough to discourage most men from availing themselves of the captain's open door. To avoid a similar situation, the teacher must analyze her own circumstances to find the barriers to communication between herself and her pupils. The process of identifying barriers—a process which cannot succeed without the active participation of the pupils—may facilitate communication. When people become involved in a genuine attempt to reach each other, barriers of role, age, race and ethnicity are, if not destroyed, at least somewhat lowered.

Tokenism

In suburban and midwestern areas, a situation often exists which cannot, in truth, even be called desegregation. In business and industry, where the situation is intentionally arranged to protect employers from charges of discrimination, it is called tokenism. There is a standing joke among civil rights workers that the single Negro employee in a firm is placed at a desk near the main entrance, to insure that every visitor sees him immediately on entering. He must, of course, be dark-skinned enough so that there is no mistaking the fact that the firm employs Negroes. In schools, tokenism often occurs without forethought, when a single minority family moves into an all-white area. The single Oriental, or Mexican or Negro child is often made much of—by teachers and students alike. He may be elected school president or captain of the baseball team—and his popularity may be exhibited by adults as evidence that the majority children have no prejudices. It is so easy to make a "pet" of someone who is "different" without an accompanying empathic awareness of the "pet's" feelings and needs. Not long ago, the principal of a midwestern high school pointed with pride to the only Negro in his all-white school, who was "completely accepted" and who had no problems and presented no problems for others. I asked the principal about the young man's social life. "Oh, it's fine," he assured me. "He's been very happy in the school."

"Does he," I asked, "go out with girls?"

"Oh, no," said the principal. "There are no Negro girls in the school."

A high school senior who cannot go out with girls—but has no problems. How far the principal was from any feeling for the boy! Nobody had ever thought to ask that question before. Everyone was convinced, because the young man was not kicking and screaming, that he had no problems!

In another school, there were eight Anglo students in a student body of six hundred Mexican-Americans. The Latin children were eager to tell me that they had elected a non-Spanish-speaking student as president of the school. "Was he the one best qualified to do the job?" I asked. And they were crestfallen because I had not complimented them on their "tolerance."

Employers who think that tokenism is proof that they are meeting the demands of fair employment are righteously indignant when the minority community indicates it is not fooled. Perhaps these employers were once praised for their openmindedness when they elected a Negro student council president in high school.

Bussing

Bussing children a short distance from their neighborhoods has become increasingly necessary in many cities because of extreme overcrowding in the inner city schools, populated predominantly by minority children. Often, this expediency is seen as evidence that the schools are being integrated, and howls are raised on both sides of the integration issue. Those who feel that integration is a vital aspect of education see evidence that little or no integration is taking place in the receiving school. Those who oppose integration seem to fasten on the bussing issue, pointing out the horrors of a fifteen- or twenty-minute bus ride for small children. (During the 1963–64 school year, more than one-third of all school children rode busses to school, and very little protest was heard. But very few of these children were bussed for reasons associated with inter-racial contact.) Actually, school systems which bus minority children to schools that are populated by the majority group are usually not effecting integration. In fact, what happens in some of these schools is a far cry even from desegregation.

One Eastern school system lists 120 of its 600 schools as integrated. Many of the "integrated" elementary schools have Negro students who are bussed from overcrowded schools in all-Negro neighborhoods. For almost a year, the Negro children were alluded to by teachers and administrators as "the bussed-in children," until even the other children began to refer to them as an amorphous, undifferentiated block of "bussed-ins." They always arrived at school fifteen minutes after the late bell had rung and were ushered into their rooms on the third floor of the school. (All other classes had been rearranged to accommodate the white children on the first and second floors.) The Negro children stayed at school for lunch; the white children all went home. Playtime, "to relieve con-gestion," was at different times for white children and for Negro children. And the "bussed-ins" were marched out to be bussed back home ten minutes before the dismissal bell rang. At this "integrated" school, Negro and white children were as effectively separated from each other as if a Berlin wall had been constructed between them.

Desegregation and Conflict

Lack of contact and communication across group lines may result in a surface calm and absence of conflict within the school walls. There is really nothing surprising about this: conflict, after all, is a form of communication. People in conflict are saying something to each other. If the psychological space between people is large enough, they cannot reach across even to wound each other. But, while appearing to ignore each other, dominant and minority groups spread rumors and repeat denigrating lies about each other and build up a readiness to react with hostility to each other.

Recently a young mathematics teacher argued vehemently that in his junior high school, none of the children—from a variety of religious, nationality and racial groups—had difficulty relating to each other. Had the children been experiencing problems, he maintained, he would have felt the existence of tension "through his pores," so sensitive was he to moods and atmosphere in the classroom. But, he said, intergroup problems were fortunately nonexistent. It was interesting, however, that the senior high school fed by his school, and located just one block away, had problems of such magnitude and frequency that policemen were regularly assigned to patrol its corridors and incidents were repeatedly reported in the newspapers. A white boy was stabbed by one of a group of Negro boys. Gangs of white girls waylaid and attacked Negro girls. "Dirty wop" and "nigger" were among the milder epithets hurled back and forth in almost every altercation. Periodically, parents kept their children home from school, announcing publicly that they would remain home until the situation was under control. In the community, whites blamed the violence of Negroes for the incidents and Negroes contended that the provocation of whites precipitated each outbreak. The level of achievement in the senior high school was very low. This was attributed variously to a low level of aspiration in the families, low intelligence among the pupils and the uncertainty of the world situation.

When I asked the young mathematics teacher how he could account for a "no-problem" junior high school so closely associated with a multi-problem senior high school, he finally agreed that it was unreasonable to suppose that intergroup problems among youngsters develop suddenly in the interval between junior high school graduation and entrance into senior high school. In a world of anti-group feelings, it was not likely that this teacher had found his way to an island where such feelings did not exist.

3   The Multi-Group Classroom—
Integration

Integration Defined

Integration is both a goal and a process. The goal is a life situation in which people of different races, different religions and diverse national backgrounds deal with each other in realistic terms. Reaching this goal involves abandoning the stereotypes we hold of other groups and, in turn, seeing ourselves as we really are, rather than blurred by favorable or unfavorable comparisons with other groups. That is, errors about other groups, and fears and hostilities based on these errors, do not affect perceptions and interactions in a truly integrated situation.

For example, the Anglo child who believes all Ladinos carry knives may be very frightened at the possibility of an altercation with a Ladino. He may, consequently, avoid contact with Mexican-American children entirely, thereby cutting himself off from the possibility of developing good relationships. The attitude toward whites of a Negro teenager who has absorbed the myth that "any single Negro guy can whip any five white guys" may reflect both the lower-class dictum, "hit first so no one will hit you" (also held by lower-class whites), and the belief that he will inevitably emerge victor in any such conflict. A child of Puerto Rican background may think Puerto Ricans are inferior to other Americans, and may be so ashamed of his father's Spanish accent that he cuts school to avoid introducing his father to his teacher during Visitors' Week. An Indian child may suggest that a rash of locker burglaries at a recently-desegregated school is the result of "letting Indians in." (Note the relationship between this incident and the case of the Indian girl who attended an all-white school and grew up fearing Indians.) Such errors, and the feelings they arouse, tend to isolate children from new experiences, limit their aspirations, generally circumscribe their lives and play havoc with their nervous systems. In order to achieve optimal interaction based on realistic perceptions, integration must be undertaken with the realization that it is both a constant process and a goal that is never completely achieved.

Certainly, the process must begin by bringing together, within the same school and the same classroom, children of different groups. Sometimes community agencies which develop educational programs for the amelioration of intergroup relations feel it more expedient, because of the hostility between groups in the community, to work separately with each group to prepare them for coming together. Though some change in attitude can be effected in this way, experience has shown that progress is much more rapid and lasting if people learn to accept each other by interacting. In the process of "working through" their feelings about each other, and going on to solve common problems, individuals are affected much more profoundly than by working in separate groups. Once the groups are together in the classroom, the teacher can bring all her knowledge and skill to bear in diagnosing the intergroup problems and engaging the constructive efforts of all the children to define and solve those problems.

Needs and Methods

Initially, the teacher may become aware that children of different groups avoid each other. The avoidance may result from inability to see members of the other group as individuals. Children of one group may never have considered those of other groups as possible candidates for meaningful relationships. This is related to the feeling that people of certain groups have their own place in the scheme of things, and that they cannot be recognized outside of those places. For example, a white teenager accustomed to seeing Negroes only as servants may feel that there is something "wrong" with a Negro teacher, and would probably regard as preposterous the suggestion that he be treated by a Negro dentist. Johnny may say in all honesty that he has nothing against Juan, but he will be completely nonplussed if asked, "Why don't you ever invite him to your home?" It is likely that the idea has never even occurred to him. Juan may be "right" as a schoolmate, a classmate or a teammate, but never be considered as a possible after-school friend. It is the job of the skillful teacher to introduce such a thought for consideration.

The teacher may be struck by the overt hostility apparent in the classroom. Children of different groups may actually dislike each other intensely, a dislike fed by adult attitudes and misconceptions, and by unpleasant contacts with each other. The children may recount, as explanations for their hostility, incidents in which members of other groups have hurt them, physically intimidated them or hurt their feelings. It is important to understand that such incidents are almost never the cause of intergroup hostility. Rather, the child very early learns to feel about others as do the adults who are important to him. His feeling is reinforced by such obvious influences as TV shows and comic strips which stereotype minority people, and by more subtle things like beginning readers which picture only white Anglo-Saxon families and children. The anti-minority group jokes which circulate among children and adults, and even the notion that "white lies" are less reprehensible than black ones, affect anti-group feelings. And when children with such feelings come into contact with people of other groups, they often experience frustration and hurt because their own expectations and behavior contribute to the unsatisfactory experience. If they are hostile, they provoke hostility; if they avoid, they are avoided in return.

One must emphasize, however, that this pattern is more common among majority group children than among minority groups. Minority-group children are often exposed to hostility and rejection without in any way bringing it upon themselves. The pattern of prejudice and discrimination in our society exposes the minority group person to snubs, rebuffs, rejections, exclusion and sometimes physical violence, even when his personality and behavior are irreproachable. The minority child's error lies mainly in assuming that *all* majority people are capable of mistreating him. It may be true that almost every white will, at some point in a majority-minority relationship, fall back upon some form of discriminatory behavior. But the minority person may be partly responsible for fulfilling his own expectation of discrimination by his own hostility or avoidance.

Thus the integration process requires that children become aware of their behavior and the attitudes underlying it. It is not realistic to suppose that behavior and attitudes can be modified without consciously recognizing them, tracing their origins and systematically evaluating what we do and how we think. For a while, children may be reluctant and uncomfortable in discussions of intergroup problems. But with skillful encouragement in a non-punitive atmosphere they will gradually begin to talk over their own discomforts and to try to understand the sources of them. But this is not to imply that such discussion will immediately lessen tension. It may, in fact, temporarily increase the level of manifest conflict. Should conflict arise, whether violent or merely verbal, it can be used as raw material for analysis and for the development of greater understanding. A bald statement like, "Indians aren't clean," or a shove to release suppressed aggression, may cause a fight in the classroom, in the corridor or even in the street after classes are dismissed. Most teachers have had plenty of practice in separating combatants and know how to administer the first aid for such a problem. But the teacher oriented to the constructive solution of behavior problems will explore the cause of the fight with the fighters and the bystanders. Recognition of the fight's causes, as well as the opportunity to shout out grievances against the other party, may not only prevent future fights, but also pave the way for positive amicable relationships. Reconstructing the events that led up to the fight by role-playing the parts of the combatants may give the other children a chance to see clearly exactly what caused the explosion. They might then role-play alternative responses and solutions, so that fighting could be recognized as an ineffective solution. They might ultimately be able to trace the causes of the fight beyond the immediate provocation to previously unrecognized prejudices.

As unspoken feelings are brought into the open, conflict incidents may occur which seem to relate directly to the material being discussed. It must not be hastily concluded that frank discussion is the cause of the conflict. The children, uncomfortable at the growing realization that they have prejudices against their classmates, may insist that the discussion is "making" them prejudiced. If they are moved to rationalize prejudices they have long denied, they will be faced with the reactions of those who will not accept rationalizations as facts. If children feel themselves under attack, they may counterattack. But such action and reaction, if accompanied by consistent attempts to understand what is happening, can ultimately lead only to a healthier interaction between groups.

There will come a period when many youngsters will be self-conscious about discussing intergroup relations. This embarrassment differs from the children's original discomfort at confronting members of the other group face-to-face, but is not yet evidence of growing self-awareness. This self-consciousness involves an increasing sensitivity to the feelings and needs of other people, accompanied by fear that old modes of expression and old ideas may slip out inadvertently and hurt members of the other group. For example, one white Eastern high school student wanted to say that he agreed with the goals of a local civil rights demonstration. "White people have no right," he said, "to interfere with the niggers demonstrating." He was horrified and embarrassed at what he had said, but the Negro students in the class minimized the slip, reassuring him that words learned in an unthinking childhood were hard to eliminate from one's vocabulary. This class had been working for months to understand the nature of prejudice, and they had evidently developed considerable skill in helping each other to alter attitudes and patterns of behavior. During this period of self-consciousness, youngsters need understanding support from teachers and from each other. They need to realize that slips are inevitable during the learning-changing process and that fortitude and calm skill in analysis are necessary to prevent such slips from becoming bars to further communication. If an individual is hurt, for example, by the inadvertent use of the word "boy," he must be encouraged to maintain communication and not be allowed to withdraw from the discussion. The student who uses an insulting term must be helped to understand why he does so and encouraged to continue to communicate instead of withdrawing in embarrassment and fear of future slips.

In this area, as in others, some students will learn more quickly than others, and they will need tolerance and skill in helping slower learners. New children may join the class who have had no previous opportunity for frank interchange and practice in relating to other groups. It will take patience and understanding to help them participate fully in this new experience. This is what is meant when we say that integration is a continuous process, and that the final goal is never reached. We can never say with finality, "Now we are integrated, and we can go on to other matters." The constant shifting and changing of interpersonal relationships which are part of the very nature of classroom dynamics must be understood by the people involved. As relationships change, new problems occur, gaps in understanding are exposed, lapses in sensitivity may appear and new skills must be developed and practiced.

Suppose that a third-grade class has been having fruitful discussions of intergroup relations, and the teacher feels that whatever problems existed before are on the way to solution. The atmosphere is friendly and helpful, rapport between teacher and pupils is good and everyone is reasonably comfortable and productive. Suddenly there is a shifting of relationships. Jimmy comes to school one morning distraught because his best friend walked to school with the new boy instead of stopping by for him. The new boy is white. Jimmy and his best friend are colored. Jimmy refuses to do the assignment, talks back to the teacher, is reprimanded and bursts into tears. "If I was principal," he sobs, "I'd fire all the white teachers and cut out the teachers' lunchroom!" No one had known Jimmy had such feelings. The changing situation required a new focus on the integration process. Perhaps some understanding was needed of friendship, how people pick their friends, why friends make us happy and angry and how our feelings may be displaced onto innocent objects.

Another graphic example is an incident which occurred recently in a seventh-grade classroom of Negro and Caucasian children whose teacher believed her students had no intergroup problems. In the middle of the year two Cuban children, whose families had relocated from Miami after fleeing Cuba, entered the class. Several of the Negro children in the class had heard that Negroes and Cubans had been competing for service jobs in Miami, and that many Americans had been losing jobs to the refugees. (Some Negro people contend that Cubans are often preferred by employers because they are white.) Some of the white children had never before heard a Spanish accent and mimicked it. The newcomers met with other evidences of hostility. The "no-problem" class suddenly had a very obvious intergroup problem to cope with. Simple group rejection of newcomers was compounded by ridicule of those who are different and by negative attitudes transmitted by adults. The children could have been encouraged to put themselves in the place of the newcomers: "Have you ever felt alone and unwanted in a new place? What did you wish other people would do then?" They could have been enticed into learning a little Spanish from the Cuban children, and might have discussed the nature of job competition that is complicated by color prejudice.

Dynamic integration must not only deal with present relationships, but must develop in such a way that possible future relationships can be entered into without friction. It is not realistic to suppose that the group or groups we know now are the only types of people we will know for the rest of our lives. The chances are good, in a highly mobile population, that we will need to work closely with members of groups we never expected would be a part of our lives. Just as vocational and professional education must prepare children to earn their livings at jobs that are not even envisioned today, intergroup relations education must prepare them to live harmoniously with people neither they nor their parents have met.

There is a danger that learning about people from other parts of the world can become a mere exercise in the appreciation of the "exotic," and traditional intercultural education units may be used as a substitute for dealing with everyday intergroup relations. It is wiser and more important to develop sensitivity to people we perceive as different from ourselves by starting with the people closest to us, and gradually extending our understanding to those more and more remote from us.

As misconceptions about other groups are eliminated, students become aware of similarities between their own groups and others. At this point, they may be encouraged to explore and develop common school goals, as well as the broader life goals they share. They will begin to see that the similarities among people far outweigh the differences, and that strength and satisfaction are to be found in working together for common goals.

To sum up, "integration" is an active, changing learning situation which involves children of different groups in a process of knowing each other and living with each other. It is not a static "bull's eye" target, but a dynamic life process which never ends.

4 The Teacher

Teachers' Special Skills

Most teachers have very little factual information about race, minority-group history, religions other than their own or the psychology of intergroup relations. This is not surprising, for their own teachers undoubtedly knew even less. They may have taken a single college course in group sociology. Their professional education, though it may have included courses in child development and educational psychology, probably ignored the aspects of these fields related to minority-group problems and the effects of group status on learning. Now the modern teacher finds herself confronted by social change which forces her toward greater awareness of intergroup problems, blames her for many of them and demands that she concern herself with mitigating their effects. It is pointless to rush defensively into self-protective postures when people shout blame at the teaching profession. Nothing productive is achieved by a "No, I'm not!", "Yes, you are!" argument. The wisest course is simply to recognize that our society has inherited this social situation and that all of us have a responsibility to improve it.

Moreover, those who expect teachers to take on a major part of the job are not being unreasonable. Teachers are uniquely equipped to effect changes in behavior and attitude and to accept the challenges of difficult educational situations. Although the teacher—like the rest of the population—is a product of our society, the nature of her specialized education implies a responsibility to search beyond conventional ignorance to the available scientific knowledge. She learns very early to discount what "they say" and "everybody knows," and to look for more authoritative bases for her opinions. Teachers also have been trained to search out facts. Remember the endless research to collect facts for term papers? This is what those papers were all about! And every year of teaching children to search for facts, evaluate authorities, differentiate fact from opinion and to reach workable conclusions on the basis of available knowledge should have reinforced our original training.

We are sophisticated enough to know that complete objectivity is a myth. There are factors in the lives of all of us that make absolute objectivity impossible. In regard to ethnic and racial groups, it is the rare researcher who can free himself from his internalized social frame of reference. In our society, we are exposed from childhood to misconceptions about other groups which are generally denigrating. These misconceptions constitute predispositions to accept certain facts and reject others. For example, most people can accept as fact that the religion of the Jews places a high value on erudition, which serves them well in a society which bases "getting ahead" on education. But it is not as widely accepted a fact that Jews are not by birth "cleverer" than other people.

Also, most English-speaking Americans know very well that there are wide variations among them in the readiness to accept work as a social value. But most find it difficult to recognize that there are equally wide variations among Spanish-Americans.

And again, Americans of European background commit crimes for many reasons, among them anti-social behavior learned from adults, limited behavioral alternatives in their lives, inability to cope with frustration and fear of investing themselves in the future because of present financial and emotional insecurity. Research confirms these hypotheses. But when Indian-Americans commit crimes, many whites refuse to recognize that the same causes result in the same behavior. In the minds of most whites, Indian crimes are somehow linked to hereditary and ethnic factors. Similarly, Negroes, as aware as they are of the multiplicity of individual differences in their group, are often skeptical about evidence of differences among whites, especially in the area of intergroup attitudes and behaviors.

The inability to accept certain facts is related to our very early learnings. We all know children who will not accept certain information because they have learned otherwise at home. The child whose parents tell him that bulls see red may be skeptical when told at school that bulls are color blind, even though he is unlikely to be strongly committed emotionally to the belief that bulls see colors. But if one is taught at home, for example, that Japanese-Americans use unfair methods to put "real" Americans out of business, one will tend to resist recognizing that Japanese-Americans and other Americans display pretty much the same business behavior. This is especially true if the child lives in an area of the country where there are many Japanese businessmen. If his father is also a businessman, the resistance is compounded. Accepting the truth and rejecting the initial misconception involves the child in a number of disturbing corollary steps, like questioning his father's ability to succeed in business. Intergroup misconceptions are emotionally linked to the need to believe in mothers and fathers who had the same misconceptions. To relinquish these errors often involves re-evaluation of one's self and one's world.

Do you remember when it was first suggested to you, perhaps in an education class, that your parents' way of disciplining their children was not necessarily the best way? How ready were you then to examine this idea? Or did you leap to your parents' defense—pointing to yourself as evidence of the soundness of their methods? But the scientific training of teachers, their insistence that pupils learn facts and their respect for authoritative research stand them in good stead here. If anyone can rise above the inbred inability to deal rationally with emotionally-toned facts, the teacher can. It is not easy to step back a pace from ourselves and watch our emotions interfering with our rationality. We human beings prefer to think of ourselves as rational creatures, and it takes maturity to admit that most of our judgments are clouded by our feelings.

Intergroup feelings affect not only our acceptance or rejection of facts, but also our acceptance or rejection of people in everyday relationships. For example, why do few white people have Negro friends? Is it only because they have been reared apart from Negroes? Or is it also because they overlook and avoid opportunities to make friends among Negroes? What is the feeling of a non-Spanish-speaking woman when she sees a man of obviously Latin background walking toward her on a deserted street? Is she afraid? Would she be as afraid if the man were obviously non-Latin? When a Negro child disobeys, is the white teacher angrier than she would be at a disobedient white child? And the Negro teacher—does her reaction to the misbehavior of a Negro child reflect a fear of failure or need for acceptance by whites? Does the Mexican-American teacher view with skepticism the friendly overtures of her non-Spanish colleagues? Does the Negro teacher eat lunch alone to avoid risking the rebuff she expects from white teachers?

Such feelings may not completely disappear even when the teacher is able intellectually to reject old misconceptions and accept new facts. There is often a dichotomy in our responses: we may accept certain truths intellectually while we still reject them emotionally in favor of our old misconceptions. We may begin to associate with people of other groups but still feel uncomfortable, frightened or nervous in their presence. But practice and familiarity weaken such feelings. And, if we continue to be honest about our difficulties and judiciously evaluative of our own behavior, we may be able to help our pupils develop a similar honesty and sensitivity to others.

If the teacher really does want to know how people feel, she must embark upon planned action to learn, just as she did to earn her bachelor's degree. First, she needs facts. They can help her to expand and deepen her awareness of how people think and what they feel about intergroup matters—all people, not just members of her own group. And she must begin to listen to other people. If she is of the majority group, she may listen to Negro commentators and read novels, poems, stories and essays by minority writers—a superb way to listen in a psychologically safe atmosphere. She must listen to the children she teaches and, as much as possible, to their parents. She must open her mind to listen without recriminations, signs of rejection or devaluation of what she hears. For feelings are facts, and no amount of recrimination will change the fact that the feelings she hears expressed exist. She knows that familiarity with people's feelings undergirds any approach to teaching new behavior and attitudes.

Intergroup Skills

But knowledge and sensitivity alone are not enough. The teacher must develop the special skills which will enable her to *use* her knowledge and reflect her sensitivity. She must be able to work with people of other groups without experiencing acute discomfort based on group differences. This skill takes most of us a long time to develop. Our experience with people of other groups has, as a rule, been very limited. We may have had an employer-employee relationship with someone of another group. We may have sat in class next to a student of another group, or played on a ball team with one. Some of us have served on committees with members of other groups. But rarely have our contacts been the sustained, equal-status relationships which two people of the same group develop. The idea of race or religion or national origin has been a wall between us and another person, making us uncomfortable in each other's presence, fearful of saying or doing the wrong thing, hoping the contact would end as soon as possible, relieving us of the obligation of being with someone we dislike or fear, or even hate—someone who may say something to hurt us or whom we may inadvertently hurt. Though knowledge and sensitivity help in overcoming such discomfort, there is no substitute for continued practice of the skills involved in relating to people of other groups.

We must, of course, learn not to use words or terms which members of other groups find offensive. Many people who maintain that they never employ racial or religious epithets are surprised to learn that words like "boy," when used to describe a minority-group man, and expressions like "I jew him down" imply prejudice, or at least gross insensitivity, to minority-group people. A majority-group person may protest that he "didn't mean anything" by his choice of words, or that "we always use that expression." But such terms originated in stereotypic thinking and discriminatory behavior, and the sensitive person will recognize the hurt and anger they evoke and will eliminate them from his vocabulary.

Similarly, the knowledgeable and sensitive minority-group person will understand that majority people learn such words before they are able to reason and judge for themselves, and will find the courage and skill to overlook slips by people who are trying to abandon old habits of thought.

Ideas, as well as words, intrude between people of different groups to cause misunderstandings and impede communication. The white person who tells a casual Negro acquaintance, "You people need more agreement among yourselves," immediately constructs a barrier to further friendship. The phrase "you people" implies that Negroes as a group function according to special rules in a milieu unconnected to the speaker's world. And the implication that the speaker is qualified to diagnose the needs of that other world is highly presumptuous. I have never understood why whites, themselves so divided in loyalties, opinions and points of views, should be surprised that twenty million Negro people do not think alike, act alike and join the same organizations. It is remarkable how many white people continue to stereotype Negroes as all alike in the face of so much evidence that Negroes are as individualized as whites.

It has become fashionable for majority people to respond to minority demands for equality by assuming an air of stern objectivity. "We must not encourage minority people to use accusations of prejudice as a crutch," they say. The implication of such a statement is that instead of working hard and "proving himself" worthy of acceptance, the minority person prefers to fail and to blame his failure on prejudice.

Those who make such diagnoses, though they present themselves as ruthlessly objective, are engaging in a neat bit of rationalization. The inescapable fact is that most majority-group people are prejudiced. It is also true that most of us are unaware of the subtle ways in which our prejudices influence our judgments. When a minority person complains of prejudice, we would do well to listen carefully and to examine the allegation diligently before writing it off as an excuse for failure.

The idea that minority people are obliged to "prove themselves" is the direct antithesis of the prevailing American philosophy. We pride ourselves on accepting a person unless he does something to betray our acceptance. Our laws and historical documents express our conviction that men are created equal and are innocent until proven guilty. We are known around the world as friendly people, open and informal with strangers. And yet, paradoxically, we insist on "proof" from some of our fellow citizens.

In the classroom, particularly, the teacher needs to develop skill in evaluating youngsters without being influenced by preconceptions founded on their group membership. The teacher's ability to gauge a child's potential and progress is vital to the child's continuing development. The beliefs that Indian children are always stoic, that Mexican-American children are lazy, that Negro children are undisciplined and Jewish children academically gifted blind the teacher to her students' real needs and prevent her from offering them adequate opportunity to do their best. Convinced that Negro children are undisciplined, the teacher may be overly harsh with a restless Negro child and much more tolerant of the same behavior in a white child. To regard someone as lazy is to make a moral judgment, and the teacher may make obvious her contempt for the Mexican-American child who—like the non-Spanish child—neglects his homework one night. Such judgments are not realistically attuned to the individual child; they are based on figments of the teacher's imagination, and thus may interfere not only with the child's development, but also with the teacher's professional fulfillment.

Above all, the teacher must continue her associations with individuals who have less skill and sensitivity than she in relating to people of other groups, and must help them to develop such skill. Her colleagues, supervisors and administrators can all benefit from what she has learned in her endeavor to improve her own intergroup relations. This is essentially what she sets out to do with her pupils when she decides to make intergroup relations education an integral part of her teaching—to help them to benefit from her own struggles.

But how do you teach something you are not expert at yourself? Fortunately, this is no problem for the skillful teacher. She already knows that in the process of teaching a subject she becomes more and more knowledgeable. In the process of preparing materials and gauging her students' reactions to them, she becomes increasingly sensitive to her students' needs and skillful in providing for them.

There is no doubt in my mind that a good teacher is eminently qualified to teach intergroup relations, to fill the gaps in understanding left by parents and to change the misconceptions fostered by society. She is skilled in gathering knowledge, sensitive to individual needs and able to communicate what she has learned. Once teachers realize the relevance of intergroup education to individual and social needs, it is likely that we will finally have begun to solve our most pressing social problem.

III

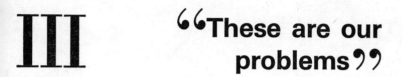

"These are our problems"

5 Intergroup Problems of Middle-Class Majority Children

Isolation

Most middle-class white English-speaking children live in an overwhelmingly white middle-class English-speaking world, and rarely escape it. They go to neighborhood schools, where they meet other white middle-class children. Their parents' friends and acquaintances are also white and middle-class. In most parts of the country, the minority-group person never enters a white home as a friend—for dinner, a party or a visit. What contact the white child has with people of other groups is not the relationship of equals. He may know minority-group people who work for his and his neighbors' families, but this kind of relationship does not allow for the free exchange of ideas and feelings or for the spontaneous behavior which occurs among equals. Thus the white child is deprived of a vast and vital area of human experience.

Inevitably, the majority person will be obliged to make equal-status contact with minority people as he grows farther away from his home and neighborhood. In his profession he will probably have to work side by side with members of other groups. He may have to consult experts in his field who are not of his own racial group. He may find himself living in a neighborhood with people of a variety of racial and ethnic backgrounds. How comfortable will he be in such situations? How effectively will he be able to communicate with people about whom he harbors fears and resentments? How fruitful can his associations be if they are undermined by all kinds of misconceptions? (As we shall see in the next chapter, minority children educated in segregated circumstances encounter the same difficulties when they are compelled to live and work in equal-status situations with majority-group children. Here, too, negative feelings and erroneous beliefs get in the way of productive relationships.)

Most majority people who grow up in this kind of isolation rarely question what is happening to them. What self-questioning they do tends to take the form of rationalization or self-justification. "Why shouldn't I live among my own kind of people?" they ask. I am not suggesting here that people should not be permitted to live among the people they view as most like themselves. But such a choice should be freely made, with full awareness of the possible alternatives. If a person grows up ignorant of other people and other ways of life, the choice he makes is no choice at all. He lives as he does because he knows no other way. A major goal of the educational process in a democratic society should be to excite pupils with the prospect of a life whose rich possibilities are limited only by their own knowledge, curiosity and imagination.

If the school is to fulfill its responsibility to help people broaden their perspectives and live fuller lives, it must help children to understand the pressures in our society toward isolation and prejudice and to resist those pressures. Does the child have enough confidence in himself to risk standing up for an unpopular point of view? Does he have the skill to identify people who feel as he does and is he able to join forces with them? Does he have some understanding of the needs for authority, conformity and independence which may move people to resist him or agree with him? Above all, is the child as competent in recognizing and using facts about other individuals and groups as he is in dealing with people? We all know of people whose skill in persuasion and argument often involves outright lying, and whose perception of the world is a hodgepodge of fantasy and inaccuracy.

The child who needs to obtain group acceptance by denigrating others is alone in a hostile world, for he will never find a satisfying kind of acceptance. His attacks on other people will become more and more virulent as he becomes less and less sure of his own position and feeling of worth. The child who smugly parrots, "Everyone knows Indians are dirty," needs at least as much remedial attention as does the child who writes on an English composition, "They have all went home." Why is it that most English teachers would cringe at the second statement and disregard the first? Which statement is more dangerous? Which can wound another person, help deprive him of opportunity or demean his conception of himself? And, when school is out and we have all "went home," which has done the most permanent harm?

In a world as diverse as ours, the American white middle-class child is truly disadvantaged. His world is circumscribed, and his friends are mirror-images of himself. He must spend his life denying the value of variety, lest he be forced to conclude that his own existence is narrow and deprived. He must expend energy avoiding association with people different from himself, lest he "dilute" his own purity. But, above all, he will live and die ignorant of all the people and things on earth that exist outside of his own small bastion. His decisions and his judgments will be based on limited knowledge and experience, and consequently will be of limited validity. His associations, based primarily on uniformity of skin color and ethnic background, will deprive him of potential friendships. And his children, if they are reared in the same environment, will perpetuate the cycle of deprivation.

Stereotyping

The essential intergroup problem of most middle-class white children—or, more accurately, middle-class children of the majority group—is that they do not see minority people as real people. Whether it is the Negro porter or the Mexican farm worker, the majority-group child sees him through a haze of misconception and limited experience. He is perceived as a one-dimensional figure. Their limited contact with people of other groups often allows majority children to persist in believing that minority-group people are all satisfied with their lot in life, that they love their employers and are childishly grateful for small favors. Majority children tend to assume that all minority people have the same occupations and the same traits, uniquely suited to their low status. The Negro physician, the Mexican teacher or the Japanese architect are almost impossible for them to visualize. Witness the child who observed aloud that the only Negro child in her elementary school was probably the daughter of a maid. Her mother nodded in agreement. There was no intentional malice in the child's observation, only profound error and ignorance. The fact was that the Negro child's father was an engineer who lived in the town. But the white child and her mother were both unfamiliar with Negroes in any but the most menial occupations. Such innocent error can have evil effects. Each time a person makes such an error, he mentally consigns millions to lives not of their own choosing. He says, in effect, "You don' belong here, you belong there. Be sure to stay in your place. The white, middle-class children who make these innocent errors will grow up to own businesses, buy homes, vote for government officials and serve on school boards. The child who grows up to own his own business will turn away qualific people because he cannot imagine them in any jobs but those that have traditionally been considered Negro jobs or Chinese jobs or Mexican jobs. He will see and evaluate not the real person, but a stereotype that exists only in his mind. The white adult who shops for a home will refuse to live next door to a Chinese-American, not because he dislikes the individual, but because he thinks the Chinese-American's home has a "place" elsewhere, out of sight of the white person's home. The white voter will see no "place" in government for the Indian politi cian. And the white school board member will think the Negr child has no "place" in a school with white children.

Some time ago, the movie "Pressure Point" depicted a young man who had gotten into trouble with the law. In prison, he was assigned to a psychiatrist for treatment. When he was admitted to the psychiatrist's office by a Negro, th young man was dumbfounded. *"You're* the psychiatrist?" he asked in amazement. In his image of doctors, he could see no place for a Negro. A Negro bootblack would have been accepted without question.

How must it feel to meet someone who has made up his mind about you before he even hears your name? What a feeling of discouragement and hopelessness must overwhelm some people when they look into another person's eyes and get no answering look of recognition! As teachers, we know what it is to be stereotyped. We know how it feels to be seen as a "frustrated, embittered old maid," or as someone who settled for teaching because she couldn't *do* anything or who is so accustomed to ordering children around that she domineers adults in the same way. People often expect us to behave like the images they have of us, and even refuse to recognize that our range of motivations is as wide as their own. *We* know we are not all alike. But many people see our individual differ ences as mere exceptions to a stereotype.

As we have noted, people who think in stereotypes are likely to find it very easy to isolate the "rare exception" from is group and make a pet of him. Thus, it is in schools populated by white middle-class children that we see one or two minority children being petted and fussed over by the majority students, and often by teachers as well. They are given prestige positions, are indulged when other children would be reprimanded and are made to feel special in a way that makes ordinary human relationships impossible for them. This phenomenon may be, in part, a result of conscious attempts by some majority-group people to prove to themselves and others that they are not prejudiced. The contention of white adults that children do not think about such things as color and prejudice is disproved by this kind of compensatory behavior. It often seems as if majority people are moved by guilt to make pets of occasional minority individuals. It seems that we are trying to deny the existence of the "dilemma" Gunnar Myrdal recognized in us: the conflict between our profession of belief in democracy and our undemocratic treatment of some segments of our population.

Delusion

It is very interesting to observe the consummate skill some white middle-class people have developed at fooling themselves. The middle-class mother who says, "I know there are colored children in Johnny's class, but I can't tell from his conversation which ones they are," is convinced that her Johnny has no prejudice. But Johnny never talks about sex either, and that doesn't mean he has no feelings or curiosity about it. Perhaps Johnny has learned that there are some things you just don't talk about with adults.

Similarly, a high school student may feel that, because he is friendly to the Spanish-American students on his baseball team, he is not prejudiced. He would not think of double-dating or of inviting one of them to his home, and he rarely eats lunch with any of them. But he is "not prejudiced." And for the rest of his life he is likely to counter every suggestion of self-appraisal with an account of this experience in intergroup "acceptance." "I went to school with them. We played on the same team. Why, there was one of them—he was a very good friend of mine." Even the words he chooses—"one of them", "with them"—betray a feeling of distance that belies the apparent sentiment.

The delusion persists that whites have no prejudices, that all Americans share equally in the benefits that America has to offer. If minority people obviously do not have many of the material goods by which we measure prosperity, it is—many whites maintain—their own fault. If they want more money, they ought to get better jobs. (But Negroes are turned away from better jobs!) If they want decent homes, they ought to save their money and buy them. (But Mexican-Americans are denied the opportunity to buy decent homes even if they can afford them. Banks often refuse them mortgages readily available to other Americans!) But whites are not prejudiced; some of their best friends are Negroes!

Nor is this the only aspect of the delusion. The world is, after all, not predominantly white and middle-class. It is mostly colored and poor, and the voice of the majority is beginning to be heard. The Chinese in Hong Kong, long considered by the whites of Hong Kong as a calm and docile people, are rioting in the streets and demanding fair treatment. Starving people in India are throwing rocks at their politicians. And revolution is brewing among the oppressed black people of South Africa. Yet white middle-class people continue to function in a fantasy world in which they are not only right but also in the majority. Such delusion is dangerous, because the real world will inevitably intrude upon the fantasy.

White Power

The white middle class has, for a long time, defined the dominant styles, values and associational patterns of American life, and has excluded from the mainstream those who do not conform. For three hundred years, opposition to this white monopoly has been increasing. New models of beauty have emerged, divergent cultural values have become part of our society and patterns of association are slowly modifying. Yet the old standards remain intact and contribute to growing explosiveness among the millions of the world who suffer because of them. We preach that cleanliness is in some way associated with uprightness and morality while we force millions to live in dirty poverty. We extol the virtues of the "wide open spaces" while we draw an ever-tighter noose around crowded ghettos. We say ambition is the mark of a man while we destroy some men's ambition by denying them any chance of improving their lives. As long as we impose such frustrating conflict on so many people, we are living in a world that will sooner or later explode around us.

Militant Negro leaders are not wide of the mark when they declare that the most difficult job in improving intergroup relations must be done among white people. And when they urge white liberals to concentrate their efforts on educating and organizing whites, they are defining the intergroup problem more realistically than most whites ever have. It is middle-class white children who need the most intense education in intergroup relations if our society is to progress. Whites will continue to outnumber other groups in the United States for some time. By reason of sheer numbers alone, they will hold most of the key positions, dominate policy-making and control most communications media. If whites continue to exclude minority-group people from key positions, we can no longer delude ourselves into believing that we are a practicing democracy. In a world beset with problems and flooded with innovations, everyone must pull his own weight. We cannot afford to waste the potential of any of our citizens. As national policy, it is stupid; as a pattern of human relationships, it is cruel. Who is so wise that he can take it upon himself to decide that some shall live freely and others shall not, that some men shall be free to determine their own destinies and others shall have their destinies thrust upon them at birth? Yet every employer who says, "We're not ready for integration here," and every teacher who thinks, "There's no use trying to teach some things to these people; they just can't learn much," is making a white, middle-class decision to limit another human being's potential.

6 Intergroup Problems of Middle-Class Minority Children

Differential Problems of White and Colored Minorities

The history of some white minority groups in the United States graphically illustrates the different problems faced by whites and coloreds. Immigrants from eastern and southern Europe have responded differently to prejudice and discrimination than have Negroes, for example. The children of immigrants often suffered from feelings of alienation, caught in a no-man's-land between rejection of their parents' culture and discriminatory treatment by the dominant American society. They were often ashamed of the speech patterns, food and religion of their families and hoped by rejecting them to erase the stigma of foreignness.

The third and fourth generations seem, however, to be free of a sense of stigma. They have no accents and some of their names have been Anglicized. Middle-class status has brought varying degrees of acceptance, depending upon their religion, country of origin and the region of America in which they live. Interest and pride in the traditional customs are often superimposed on the "American" pattern of living. Generally, the descendant of recent European immigrants can say honestly that he is not discriminated against in housing, employment or education.

The colored American, however, is more visible, and cannot "melt" into the general population. He finds that, though his ancestors have been in America much longer than those of most European-Americans, though he has no accent and though his way of life is "mainstream" American, he is still discriminated against.

Some whites profess to object only to impoverished, apathetic, unemployed minority people. They insist that, if these people made the necessary effort to improve their condition, they would not only benefit economically, but would also find themselves living in a country free of prejudice and discrimination. Middle-class minority people are often torn between wanting to believe that whites mean what they say and not quite believing it. The result, for many, is behavior which outdoes white, Anglo-Saxon middle-class conventionality. And this behavior is usually accompanied by fear that, no matter how much like the white middle class one acts, acceptance will still be withheld.

Middle-class Negro children, for example, are often made so sensitive to the anti-Negro stereotype in our society, that they are compelled, in many ways, to deny their Negroness. This unrealistic self-image causes them serious problems which are reflected in their interpersonal relations. Witness the young Negro mother who was sending her child off to kindergarten for the first time. She dressed the little girl carefully in starched and ironed clothes, and counseled her as she waited for the school bus, "Now remember, do everything the teacher tells you to do. Be nice to the other children. If they want a toy you're playing with, give it up. Don't cry. Always say please and thank you. Don't make any noise. Be sure to keep yourself clean." And so on.

The child nodded, wide-eyed and solemn, at each exhortation, her entire four-year-old being straining to understand what was expected of her.

After the child had gone, I asked her mother, "Why? Why all these unrealistic demands for perfection? She's only four years old. What do you expect of her?"

"She's colored," her mother answered grimly. "Most of the other children in the class are white. She's got to be twice as good as they are."

This overcompensation is the backlash of anti-Negro prejudice: whites say Negroes are dirty; we will be cleaner than whites. Whites say Negroes are violent; we will never raise our voices. Whites say we are primitive; we will never lose our tempers.

The standards of behavior that middle-class minority people set for themselves and for their children are consequently often unrealistic, rigid and over-conforming. They are also psychologically harmful in that each time the standard is not met—and such failures are inevitable—the person feels guilty and unworthy. The middle-class Negro child, fearful of being stereotyped, often ties up much of his psychic energy in maintaining conformity. He may watch other people to detect what they really think of him and agonize over the breaches in his armor. Much of the energy that should go into spontaneity, creativity and just plain pleasure in living is thus diverted into the effort to prove to himself and to the rest of the world that he does not fit the prevailing stereotype of Negroes.

Prejudice and Non-Participation

The constant struggle to achieve an impossible perfection takes its toll in other ways. There develops a need to actively dissociate oneself from any connection with those who are imperfect. Even charitable or social service associations may be avoided, for fear of being identified with the people one helps. Thus, when concern for the "disadvantaged" and economically deprived became the focus of community programs and professional education, many middle-class minority people found themselves too acutely uncomfortable to take part in such programs. This is illustrated by the response of a Negro graduate student in Education who found herself in a course that explored the problems of urban ghetto children. "I'm tired of hearing about all the things that are wrong with Negroes!" she exploded one day. "You would think all Negroes were the same. You look at me as if I'm disadvantaged, too, as if I have the same things wrong with me that those people out there have!"

It is undoubtedly true that many of her fellow students found it difficult to distinguish between Negroes of different social classes. But she, too, overgeneralized in her evaluation of the other students and of the course readings and lectures. She was convinced that the speakers, writers and other students were speaking of *all* Negroes, and that she was being identified with social disorganization, apathy and cultural impoverishment. This conviction kept her from viewing objectively the plight of the people in the ghetto. She could not bring herself to join in efforts to help solve some of the problems of the ghetto Negro, and finally left the course angry, hurt and consumed by feelings of guilt.

Many middle-class Negroes have removed themselves from the fight for equality for similar reasons. They turn away from the plight of poor people and isolate themselves in their own neighborhoods, professions and social pastimes. The physician keeps his practice limited to middle-class patients by the location of his office and the size of his fees. The teacher sends her children to a private school. The housewife opposes bussing youngsters from the inner city to the desegregated school in her suburban neighborhood. Often they are reluctant to take stands on controversial issues, especially when it would mean opposing majority white opinion and allying themselves with poor Negroes.

One might say that white middle-class people do the same things to increase their incomes, raise their status and protect themselves and their children from disadvantaging situations. Do not most Americans define ambition and success in just these terms? But minority-group middle-class Americans more often expend much time and energy running from their minority-group identification. This is particularly lamentable because they are perhaps uniquely qualified by their own experience of discrimination to help those whom it has more severely handicapped. But, afraid that their democratic, middle-class, American identity will be submerged in their minority identity, they give up this concern. Like other Americans who, for different reasons, ignore injustice, middle-class Negroes are left with deep feelings of guilt.

Intra-Group Prejudice

The minority-group person is thus often in conflict with his own feelings, fearing identification with the stereotype and even hating that in himself which makes him a part of the minority group. He sees something of himself in other members of his group who are poor or uneducated or in trouble with the law, and at the same time denies this bond. Thus, the middle-class Negro may find it difficult to deal realistically with the causes of the poor Negro's economic and social situation, and may even defend the tradition of blaming the individual fully for his own plight. This feeling may take the form of resentment of minority-group individuals whose behavior or condition seem to justify white prejudice. Thus, some Negro policemen are harsher with Negro suspects than they are with whites suspected of similar crimes. Similarly, Negro teachers sometimes set impossible standards for poor Negro children, and in many ways demonstrate their contempt for youngsters who do not measure up to middle-class standards of appearance and behavior.

(It cannot be repeated too often that most majority people are not, themselves, particularly well equipped to view realistically poverty and its accompanying behaviors. They also prefer to overlook the social forces that mitigate against success in our society. If they were ever to admit that most Negroes do not have the same access to the means of success as do whites, they would be compelled to do something about it. If they were ever to admit that a Negro man's ability and personality often do not weigh at all in the balance against his race, most whites would have to change a whole behavior pattern.)

The minority person's antagonism to lower-class members of his own ethnic group is more severely and directly self-destructive than is the majority person's attitude. A large part of his hostility is directed against himself, for being a member of a minority and for turning against his own people.

The middle class minority child needs to see himself realistically if he is to resist the pressures to model his behavior on the cracked base of anti-minority stereotypes. He (just like the white child) needs to be reminded that there is no intrinsic good in being white. The advantage comes from injustices built into the social order. The Mexican-American who confides in an Anglo, "My people are backward," is begging to be accepted because he does not fit the Anglo's image of Spanish-Americans. He is, in effect, agreeing that the stereotype is accurate, but insisting that he is an exception to it, an attitude not unlike the prejudice of majority groups. The Indian who shrugs, "There's no point in bringing up the matter of equality. It just annoys whites and doesn't change the situation," is giving up his right to "annoy" those who discriminate, in favor of a measure of surface acceptance for himself.

There is the story of a young man who came to a northern city from a southern Appalachian town when he realized that coal mining was dying in Appalachia and that the only alternatives were slow starvation, relief or the city. The day he arrived, he met a young waitress with whom he became friends. Over a period of time, she helped him find employment agencies, and eventually encouraged him to go back to school. After two years, he took a civil service test and became a laboratory technician in the city's health department. He no longer spoke of himself—half in pride and half in humility—as a "country boy." His southern accent disappeared from his speech, and if he sometimes missed the unpolluted air and easy pace of home, he never spoke of it.

When the city government set up a health center in an area of the city inhabited largely by people from the Appalachian region, the young man began to hear comments and discussions by his co-workers about the "hillbillies" they treated. When health workers railed against their stupidity at not seeking medical help, the young man never found the courage to tell them of the Puritanical stoicism that made his people closemouthed in the face of pain. When his co-workers called the southerners dirty, pointing to the trash that littered their streets, the young man failed to point out to them that trash did not pile up in the open spaces of the country as it does in crowded cities, and that the people needed time to realize this. When the health workers mocked their accent and strange vocabulary, he never protested that the language had the flavor of ancient England, modified by isolation from the mainstream of American society. Instead, he suffered with the fear that his own background would be discovered. And finally, to guard against discovery, he began to laugh louder and longer at the "hillbillies" than anyone else. Thus someone who might have contributed to mutual understanding, because he knew both the southerners and the northerners, was frightened by the intensity of prejudice into joining the majority.

7 Intergroup Problems of Poor Majority Children

Minority-Group WASPS

We ordinarily think that white Protestants of Anglo-Saxon background all belong to the majority group whose attributes and values constitute "the American Way." Actually, there are white Anglo-Saxon Protestants in America who are by every definition minority-group people. The southern Appalachian migrants, one of whom we discussed in Chapter 6, are such a group.

Another group that falls into this category are migratory farm workers, who travel from community to community as the local crops ripen to help with the harvest. It is not unusual for migrant children to work side by side in the fields with their parents; few communities seem to care enough about their education to enforce compulsory school attendance laws for migrants. Often these children are automatically blamed for all the juvenile acts of vandalism and mischief in the area, while little or nothing is done by the community to provide them with constructive or interesting leisure-time activities.

It is commonly said that migratory workers are incapable of any other way of life. They are considered shiftless by the very communities which rely on their hard work for economic survival. They are called dirty by the employers who provide substandard, rundown housing and facilities for them. They are called uneducable by people who have made no genuine effort to find ways of motivating them educationally. (If the migrants are Spanish-speaking, all the problems of isolation and rejection are compounded; they are regarded not only as undesirable outsiders, but also as foreigners.)

However, the few communities that have decided to change their patterns of interaction with the migratory workers have been gratified to find them able and eager to learn, and willing to make significant contributions to the welfare of the community. Migrant children attend school in these communities, even if only for the short time they are in the area. Some join 4-H clubs and other young people's organizations and teach the youngsters of the town something about what they learn in their travels. A few communities encourage migrant mothers to visit clinics and to learn how to maintain their families' health. (But in many more areas, health facilities are closed to "outsiders".)

Such minimal opportunities give migrant workers hope of a better future. And higher expectations have in turn led to demands for decent wages, adequate living conditions and educational facilities for their children which are increasingly being heard, and met, across the country.

Poor Non-Spanish-Speaking Whites

One prevalent pattern of prejudice in the United States is antagonism among people who are themselves victims of discrimination to groups they consider their inferiors. This is often characteristic of second-generation Europeans who live in ethnically homogeneous neighborhoods, usually contiguous to Negro neighborhoods. They are very often Catholics, which qualifies them for membership in two minorities. (Insofar as a stereotype of the Catholic still persists in our society, Catholics constitute a minority group. Although we have had a Catholic President, the campaign was not without vicious anti-Catholic activity, including the bombardment of voters with scurrilous lies about Catholic plots. Though most Catholics experience little or no limitation of choice in most areas of their lives, prejudice and discrimination still arise in other areas.)

These poor white children have a problem in relating to colored children that is compounded by the peculiar nature of their own status. Because they often live quite close to other minority-group children, on the same or adjacent streets, they have much more contact with other groups than do middle-class children. They often attend desegregated schools, where the intergroup hostility they learn at home is intensified. (Such schools offer clear evidence of what can happen when intergroup problems are not recognized, and consequently no program is designed to solve them.)

Gangs, with their in-group and out-group identifications, reinforce hostile racial attitudes. The white and black youngsters, in their separate gangs, goaded by the frustrations of poverty and the irritability that accompanies crowded living conditions, often clash in open conflict.

White children reared in such an environment often insist, when the subject of intergroup acceptance is broached, that they know all about colored people, to their sorrow. Often they will admit almost proudly that they are prejudiced. But, they add, they have good reasons for their opinions. And they will proceed to recount tales of seemingly endless attacks and counter-attacks. They are convinced, and their experience corroborates them, that colored people are hostile and aggressive. Their own hostility and aggressiveness they explain as a necessary defense against unwarranted aggression. So firmly is this view held that it is often almost impossible to pursue a rational discussion with them about colored people. It would take another lifetime of harmonious experiences to undo the effect of the past.

One genuine cause of hostility between poor white people and poor black people is the real or imagined threat of competition for available jobs. This is not to say that such fear is necessarily conscious, or that people ever offer it as an explanation of their hostility. Nevertheless, there is evidence that the myth of Negro inferiority is used as a reason for keeping Negroes from certain kinds of jobs. Thus it is said that Negroes "cannot operate machines," that Mexican-Americans "wouldn't know what to do with higher wages," and that Indians are lazy. But nervous whites are never assured by these "reasons" that colored people will indeed be kept off the labor market. The fear of eventual unemployment persists, and is displaced onto those potential competitors who are most visibly different. Intergroup contact then takes place in an atmosphere of anger and rejection which encourages and exaggerates antagonism. Thus, when these whites are urged to look at Negro people, or Puerto Rican people or Indian people more realistically, the suggestion is countered with a flat, "You can't tell me anything about them! I *know* them. I lived near them all my life!"

Social Class Integration

This brings us to an aspect of integration which is not often discussed in the current controversy over equality. When the subject does arise, it is only as a tangential aspect of Negro-white integration: the educational advantages of social class integration. Middle-class parents are often fearful of the effect lower-class children will have on their children, in the belief that all lower-class behavior is undesirable, and that middle-class children will tend to assume lower-class characteristics but lower-class children will not learn middle-class behavior. Both assumptions are unwarranted.

Many characteristics of lower-class children and their parents are functionally desirable for good mental health or admirable in terms of our social values and culture. Poor children are in many ways more reality-oriented than middle-class children. I have seen middle-class children learn a list of definitions word-perfect without understanding or caring what they were learning, and I have seen lower-class children resist such "learning" to the point of staying away from school, to be enticed back to the classroom only when they were given the opportunity to relate what they were learning to their own lives.

A lower-class parent may strike his child in anger and then immediately forget the incident, with no feeling of guilt to confuse the issue or the child. A middle-class parent in a similar situation would be likely to worry for days about the harmful effects of hitting the child and cater to him extravagantly in recompense, while the youngster worries about whether his mother really loves him.

To speak of poor children as "culturally deprived" is to define culture very narrowly. Poor people share all the fundamental assumptions and values of American culture. The American dream of success is theirs, as it is their more affluent brothers'. They know that education is the path to success, just as they believe that influential and powerful friends can smooth that path. A nice home, a car and attractive clothes are all part of their goals of success. Belief in democracy and cynicism about the way it functions; conflicting desires for international cooperation and isolationism; wholehearted response to creativity, and distrust of artists—such beliefs are facets of our culture shared by rich and poor alike.

Poor children's school responses can be understood, not as cultural deprivation, but in terms of the school's failure to speak a language they understand. For, inevitably, isolated groups speak somewhat different languages and are moved by somewhat different symbols. While a middle-class child understands life in terms of privacy, extended verbal communication with adults and planned activities, the poor child experiences little privacy in the crowded home and streets. His communication with adults is largely one-way, and he learns early to obey terse commands to "Do this" and "Don't do that." And for much of his time he is left to his own devices, to amuse and care for himself without adult planning and scheduling.

The middle-class child may learn from lower-class children something about the process of coping with a world in which one must rely on oneself much of the time, handle aggressions, make choices of associates and resist the pressures that lead to trouble with the law. The lower-class child might be encouraged by middle-class children to see some value in intellectualism. He might be encouraged to express himself creatively in words, and to learn something about the possibilities for social and political involvement to effect change in his life.

Most significantly, perhaps, bringing middle- and lower-class children together leads to the sharing of experiences and perceptions which will offer them all a more complete picture of reality. For, no matter how well a child adapts to his own environment, he is handicapped in a world in which he may be precipitated into other surroundings, forced to deal with people from another class or culture or compelled to make decisions concerning the effects of another environment. To know only a part of the world, at a time when small, isolated events can have instant global repercussions, is to live dangerously: the margin of error for each decision we make on the basis of partial understanding is much too small.

Universal Needs
in Intergroup Relations

A primary goal of our vocation as teachers is to provide for children's needs. Basically, all children—and all human beings generally—have the same fundamental needs. Different children simply need different kinds of help in satisfying those needs.

Poor white children, like poor minority children, have inadequate self-concepts. They often feel inferior because their families do not possess the symbols of success visible everywhere around them, and because they experience so much failure in middle-class-oriented schools. Discouragement and unfamiliarity with the alternatives keep their aspirations low and inhibit them from achieving as much as their native capacities allow.

Poor children of all races and backgrounds are caught in a seemingly endless cycle of poverty, self-doubt, limited aspirations, lack of motivation, rationalization of failure and further poverty. If poor children can be helped to recognize that they can succeed, that the conditions of success are manageable and that they can develop skills which will enable them to achieve what they need, they can break out of the cycle of poverty. Attempts to abolish their prejudices, often a crucial part of their defenses against hopelessness and self-rejection, would be irresponsible, and probably unsuccessful, if not accompanied by an equal effort to develop the skills and motivation necessary to escape the cycle of poverty. But as long as people continue to see the world in terms of inferior and superior people and to evaluate others by their skin color, religion or nationality, they will overlook opportunities for their own development and advancement.

8   Intergroup Problems of
Suburban Children

Working-Class Suburbs

The migration to suburbia is not, as is often assumed, uniformly upper middle-class. Relatively recently, with the growth of the inner city population, skilled and semi-skilled white families began moving into suburban housing developments, bringing with them their city values and attitudes. This is a significant move for them. They come from the neighborhoods to which their parents came as immigrants and where they themselves were reared, filled with emotion at breaking strong ties and with resentment at being compelled to break those ties. But as non-white families moved into the old neighborhoods, they packed up and left. They continue to speak nostalgically of the neighborhoods they have left, neighborhoods spoiled by "the colored."

Like the older suburbs, the populations of the tract suburbs are mostly white, though they are often heterogeneous as to religion and national origin. Sometimes, however, we see areas that are as solidly homogeneous as the city neighborhoods ever were.

To the desire to escape contact with non-whites is added the drive for the status of a suburban address. The feeling of having arrived is pervasive in working-class suburbanites; the American dream has, they feel, been fulfilled. However, their style of life is usually not greatly changed in the new surroundings from what it was in the city, and often they have little more space to live in than they had in the old neighborhood. These new suburbanites often proclaim, as the most significant reason for leaving the city, the advantages to their children of the space and physical freedom afforded by suburban living. Sociologists have questioned whether this is not a socially acceptable way of maintaining white supremacy, for conversations with the people reveal that not only were they disturbed when their old neighborhoods began to change, but also that they would be even more severely disturbed if a Negro family moved into their suburb. They often cannot rationally consider the argument that such a family would probably have the same income and be of the same socio-economic level as they, so that there could be no question of neighborhood deterioration. The suggestion is countered with such emotionalism that discussion is useless. Responses generally take the form of "I know them; I lived near them all my life" and "we have a right to live where we want to." They cannot see that this right belongs to all people. "Living where I want to" implies, to them, the right to prevent others from living there as well.

Working-class suburbanites often suggest that they have moved from the city because the suburban schools are superior in facilities, in the quality of teaching and, most important, in the quality of the student body. It is generally true that city school buildings are older, less well maintained and much too small to house adequately the growing school population. Also, more city schools must make do with a larger proportion of unqualified teachers (though it must be remembered that qualification requirements are often higher in the city than in the suburbs). Schools in the most crowded areas of the city are often characterized by a rapid turnover of teachers. It is not unusual, for example, for a child to have three or four teachers during one school year. The effect on the child's sense of security, the continuity of the teaching and the subsequent level of achievement is obvious.

Probably the most important reason given for the superiority of suburban schools is the kind of children found in them, as compared to the students in city schools. Any teacher who has taught in inner-city schools with both white and non-white children knows very well that the children's behavior, quality of performance and level of achievement are generally the same for both groups. The assumption by white parents that their children are better behaved than non-whites is just not borne out by experience. They complain bitterly about the aggressiveness and violence of non-white children, implying that their own children are always the innocent victims of such aggression. But the parents of non-white children express the same fears for their children. The result, usually, is that both whites and non-whites view each other as enemies, and the chances are that many individuals in both groups carry weapons, "defending" themselves against imminent attack.

What distinguishes the suburban school is that it usually has no non-white children and, consequently, there is no opportunity for overt expression of hostility. But hostility often may become shockingly apparent if a non-white family manages to purchase a home in the tract. There may be rioting and harassment, the Negro home may be damaged and continued police protection for the Negro family may become necessary. The aspect of such an incident most significant for teachers is that most of the rioters and harassers are usually young people who are still in school. While their parents may express their anger and dismay only verbally, youngsters are encouraged by the tone of the adult bitterness to engage in physical violence.

Because the teachers and administrators have believed that their all-white schools were free of intergroup problems, these youngsters have probably had no help in coping with the violent feelings that overwhelm them. And because the violence does not occur within the school building, it is not considered a concern of the school. Indeed, strong justifications are found for keeping quiet, in the hope that the less said about it all the sooner it will blow over. The tendency on the part of the community, and of the school people as well, is to blame the disturbance on "outside agitators." But this rationalization is only partially successful, because it is usually very easy to identify as community people those who throw the stones, shout the obscenities and make the threats.

Middle-Class Suburbs
The American middle class has a wide range of incomes, attitudes and styles of life, and middle-class suburbs vary accordingly, depending on such factors as how far from the core city they are located and the professions and incomes of the residents.

Lower middle-class people are often dissatisfied with their lives, and discouraged about their prospects for improving their status. They usually have the white-collar jobs which offer least security or hope for advancement. But while they look to the future, they tend to spend the present asserting their respectability and maintaining their distance from blue-collar workers.

Because matters of status are so closely tied to feelings about minority groups, it is not surprising that resistance to Negro move-ins is strong in lower middle-class suburbs. However, since violence and "respectability" are incompatible, the resistance takes somewhat quieter forms than in working-class areas. When a Negro family moved in to one such suburb, the neighbors began to circulate a petition urging them to move out again. The new family was assured that this was not the place for them, that they would find no compatible neighbors and that they would be happier elsewhere, with their own kind. When the petition was ignored by the Negro family, the agitation died down, though one or two of the white families did decide to leave. Three years after they had moved in, the Negro family was still psychologically isolated. Where "Good morning" would have been the usual response, they received only blank stares. Because both parents worked and their only child attended high school and was busy with music lessons, they did not feel the ostracism as much as they might have. Had this been a family with small children, with the mother spending nearly all of her time in the neighborhood, it would have been an unbearable situation.

Among upper middle-class professional people, majority-minority relations are handled somewhat differently. Most of these people, though they live in largely homogeneous communities, like to think of themselves as "liberal" and "unprejudiced." Their children live in a never-never land of white, middle-class homogeneity, which often extends to religion as well. Because these children are loved, cherished, tended and in all ways carefully reared, their overt expressions of hostility are few. Because they learn early that anti-group sentiment is unfashionable, they make no anti-group comments. Because they have no opportunity to associate with other groups, they think they have no anti-group feelings.

It has become fashionable among such liberals to include in their social gatherings a Negro couple. Usually, this couple cannot be classified as family friends. They are, rather, associates from work or from some community committee. Since the other couples at the gathering are usually close friends, there is a vague aura of discomfort in the atmosphere throughout the evening. The Negro couple becomes the symbol of "good" intergroup relations. The hosts feel that they are dealing adequately with the problem of prejudice and discrimination by having a Negro couple at their home once a month or so.

But these upper middle-class people, like others who live in all-white suburbs, do little or nothing to change the traditional compact of silence in the schools on the subject of intergroup relations. These are the parents who are interested in the schools, who attend PTA meetings, who do not hesitate to telephone the principal to discuss something about the school that disturbs them. Yet they do not see the importance of filling this gap in their children's education.

The irony of this situation was impressed on me recently, when I observed a group of professionals making a real attempt to educate themselves in intergroup relations, but giving no thought to the ignorance of their children. I was asked to meet with a group of neighbors in a suburban home to lead a discussion on some aspect of intergroup relations. In the gathering were several Negro couples who did not live in the area but had been invited to take part in the discussion. In the course of the evening, the hosts' teenage son came in and joined in the discussion, to the obvious annoyance of his parents, who apologized for the intrusion. They had not, they explained, expected him back from his date so early. The young man, at one point, proudly described the one Negro girl in his class, "whom everybody likes." The comment, though not quite relevant at the time, was eagerly but unconsciously offered as evidence that this young man was as "liberal" as his parents. When I asked him if he ever saw the girl outside of school, he looked at me blankly. Apparently, none of the students in the school "liked" her enough to invite her to their homes.

Minorities in the Suburbs

Except in suburbs that are entirely Roman Catholic or entirely Jewish, the ethnic and religious hostilities apparent in cities are becoming more and more evident in the working-class suburbs. In the struggle between different groups, each fearing the domination of the other, the schools may become the battleground. This is especially apparent in the controversy over teaching religion in the public schools. The American Catholic parochial school system was established primarily to remove Catholic children from the Protestant orientation of the early nineteenth-century public school. Today, Jews, Seventh Day Adventists and Unitarians, among others, are disturbed at the religious teaching that goes on in the public schools. They fear the domination of Catholics, who very often constitute a majority of the suburban population. To avoid the danger of a majority-sponsored religion in the schools, they insist on eliminating religious teaching from the schools entirely. Most working-class Roman Catholics, at least in the suburbs, press to maintain some aspect of religious education in the public schools. In one suburb the controversy involved other factors as well. The Catholic group wanted larger classes and emphasis on the three Rs, while the Jewish group campaigned for more buildings and an expanded curriculum.

As for non-white families in the suburbs, their numbers are slowly increasing. Sometimes they make up a small "colony," isolated from any kind of interaction with the white community. They have often lived in the area for some time, and are described by the newer white residents as different from the colored people who live in the city.

Here again, the schools are insensitive to intergroup needs. In one such suburban area the high school administration explored the possibility of developing an intergroup relations program. After discussing the matter with a consultant, they decided to "let the Negro kids in the school have a jazz club." This plan was then presented to the community as an indication of good human relations in the school. The fact that Negro youngsters belonged to none of the prestige clubs in the school, that they ate lunch at a table by themselves, that they never ran for elective offices—these facts were not considered in evaluating the state of intergroup relations in the school. It was simply assumed that Negro youngsters all like jazz, and that such a club would fulfill their extracurricular needs.

Generally speaking, there is little doubt that ethnic and racial factors are as influential in the suburbs as they are in the cities. Though in the cities the proximity of various groups make tensions more apparent, the greater homogeneity of the suburbs does not hide the need for intergroup education. But this homogeneity is only a temporary condition. Undoubtedly, employment discrimination will disappear more rapidly than discrimination in any other area. The development of vast metropolitan complexes, with scattered industrial-residential sites, will inevitably encourage the heterogeneity of residential populations; and educational parks, fed from combined city-suburban areas, will give us more heterogeneous schools. Wherever we live, whatever kind of work we do, we must soon take giant steps to educate all children to live together harmoniously in the same world.

9   Intergroup Problems of Poor Minority Children

White Values

It is not just middle-class minority children who need, consciously or unconsciously, to identify with the majority group in our society. Poor Negro children sometimes reveal such needs as well. There was the ninth-grade Negro girl who wrote a note to a friend in class, apparently hoping her teacher would intercept it. "Dear Mary," she wrote, "I think Mr. Smith is cute. I think I love him because he's white. When I get married, I'll marry a white man." To love someone because of the color of his skin is as much a sickness of prejudice as hatred of a person's skin color. To cherish an ideal *because* it is different from what you are is to say, in effect, "I do not like myself." How many implications for ambition, achievement, success and happiness there are in this attitude!

The whole fabric of our society teaches minority children not to compete with the majority. Separation from majority children in school, together with lessons learned from parents who are discriminated against and older brothers and sisters who have experienced disillusion and discouragement, convinces these children that they are not as good as whites. If they are also poor, their feelings of insecurity do not permit them to have faith either in themselves or in the future. Poverty and prejudice combine to convince them of their unworthiness and inability to win in competition, and of the futility of striving for a better life. In their every act of rebellion and impertinence and in every hostile stare, poor minority children are saying to the teacher, "Aw, what the hell's the use of all this! You know as well as I do that I'm not going anywhere."

"Do you wish you were brown?" the Negro child asks the white teacher. "Everyone should be proud of his own color," the teacher sermonizes in reply. But where is this pride to come from? Perhaps the teacher might have led the child to greater self-understanding if she knew more about his feelings. "Do you wish you were white?" she might have asked, rather than discouraging him from expressing himself by telling him how he *ought* to feel. Is this child absorbing white stereotypes? Has "white" become "right" for him, and black or brown somewhat less than right? Is the prevalent white belief that black must "stay back" becoming a part of his belief? What does he know about the "rightness" of black? What do *you* know about the rightness of black that you could teach him?

School Environment

It is true that poor minority children have problems which teachers alone cannot eliminate. However, even the most crippling situation can be somewhat mitigated in the school setting. We know, for instance, that crowded conditions contribute to irritability and result in disorder. The limited accommodations available for the poor, and the difficulty minority people have finding housing outside the slums, force most poor minority children to live in extremely crowded conditions. Though the physical size of the ghetto slum does not increase much, the population continues to multiply rapidly, and conditions become more and more congested.

If a child from such an environment cannot, even during the hours he spends in school, look forward to some breathing space, an occasional quiet corner for himself and, above all, some understanding of the causes of his often impulsive and hostile behavior, we have no right to expect him to receive our pearls of wisdom with welcoming mind and heart. He is often seething with frustration, and we expect him to raise his hand before he speaks. He is often unable to find a quiet half hour to himself, and we chastise him for not doing his homework. He often lives in a world where the quest for beauty of physical surroundings has long ago been abandoned, but we imprison him in an ugly factory-like school with seats nailed to the floors and plaster peeling from the walls.

If a child has no place at home to study, we must find a quiet spot for him in school. If a child comes to school late every morning because no one at home is time-oriented, we must arrange his school life so that he can pick it up whenever he comes in—even while we are trying to teach him how to live by the clock. If a child is irritable and distracted because he comes to school without breakfast, the school must arrange to feed him, if it hopes to teach him. (What is the point of engaging in an endless "discipline" controversy with such a child, when all we have to do is give him breakfast so that we can get on with the job?))

Curriculum Factors

Just as the policeman symbolizes to the poor Negro child a hostile white society bent on destroying him, the teacher also represents a hostile authority imposing unrealistic values and demands unrelated to his needs. The elementary school teacher presents a unit entitled "The Policeman is Our Friend." But their big brothers have long ago taught the children that the policeman is someone to be avoided and that innocence is no protection against humiliation, harassment and even bodily harm. Which lesson does the child learn? The teacher cannot continue to teach lessons drawn from another world and hope to be successful. The wellsprings of learning must be found in the world of the child, and flow from there to the wider world.

Though most children are not "retarded," "dumb," "slow learners" or "low-I.Q.s" when they start out in life (or in school), it is amazing, and shameful, with what rapidity poor minority children become dumb the longer they attend school. The traditional classroom methods, largely instituted several generations ago, the attitudes and expectations of teachers and the very textbooks on which most teachers rely exclusively, all contribute to reducing the learning ability of the poor minority child. Most teachers have been warned, long before they started to teach poor minority children, of their inability and lack of motivation to learn. Even the "dedicated" teachers, who grit their teeth and resolve to do the job out of a sense of humanitarian responsibility, usually settle for a kind of desperate maintenance of order and resigned satisfaction at a minimal response. The point is that most teachers do not expect much in the way of academic achievement from poor minority children, and thus are partly responsible, perhaps unconsciously, for seeing to it that their expectations are fulfilled

Most of the frustration that teachers of poor children feel, and the prime rationale for deciding that they are stupid and unable to learn, is the fact that poor children generally do not learn very well through our customary teaching methods. Lecturing, writing occasional words on the board, drilling children and making them repeat our words, and relying heavily on reading and written lessons constitute a method that emphasizes verbal communication too much to be useful to children whose most significant development is in motor ability. These children learn best by handling physical objects and through action, and they are handicapped in a learning situation which emphasizes listening and repetition. To illustrate how we often become the agents of failure, I am reminded of the mathematics teacher in an urban junior high school made up largely of poor white children from Appalachia, some poor Negro children and three poor Indian children whose families had recently moved to the city. The teacher had been given a budget of fifteen dollars to buy materials, and had purchased an abacus and a bag of Cuisenaire rods to use for demonstrations. *But he would never permit the children to touch the equipment, because "These kids don't know how to take care of things; they'd ruin them in a minute."* But if it was true that the children did not know how to take care of things, how were they ever to learn to do so? And if they were never to be permitted to learn in the style most comfortable for them, what hope was there for them in a society that makes education a prerequisite for success?

Unappreciated Strengths

Poor Negro and other minority children can make unique contributions to our country's progress. These children are remarkably well-informed and realistic about the nature of intergroup relations in this country. They know, as only its victims can, about the white man's thinly disguised fear of Negroes. They know the white "liberal" who believes in open housing, yet falters in his belief when a Puerto Rican family moves into his own neighborhood. They are familiar with sentimental testimonials to "your people" which result in no new jobs, no new homes, no better schools. And, given half a chance, the poor minority child (and adult) will speak honestly in an interracial group about his feelings and about the intergroup situation. The poor white child is much more reluctant to express his feelings in a mixed group. It is the Negro child, more often than not, who will take the lead in openly discussing the fears, hurts, doubts and angers he feels. And though he will often laugh in derision and frustration at the naiveté and hypocrisy of whites, he learns very quickly that laughter discourages honesty of expression, and he controls it.

Too often, poor children are viewed as being so overwhelmed by deficiencies (or is it the *teachers* who are overwhelmed?) that teaching them on any kind of meaningful level is impossible. The problems are endlessly catalogued: they are undisciplined, they don't care about education, their parents don't encourage them, their verbal ability is limited, and so forth. These observations are often presented as "proof" that the teacher must settle for "maintaining order" and for seriously teaching only those few pupils who have miraculously managed to survive the pressures for non-achievement. For children of Indian, Mexican-American, Negro or Puerto Rican background, the "proof" of their inability to learn is found in heredity. It is surprising how even the most sincerely committed teachers consistently overlook the strengths of poor minority children which have kept them from succumbing totally to their environments, and which could be called upon to achieve success and fulfillment in our society.

The vocabularies of poor children often dismay the middle-class teacher, and cause him to denigrate them. Poor children use "poor" English, obscenities and words which the teacher cannot begin to decipher. How many teachers have ever thought to regard this "poor" English as a strong and unambivalent means of expression? We middle-class people have learned "tact," diplomacy with words and what our grandmothers might have called "pussyfooting." Poor children, partly because of the paucity of their vocabularies, but certainly also because they have no inclination for that kind of dishonesty, say what they mean, directly and without embellishment. If we listen to what they are saying, perhaps we will not be so quick to conclude that the words they use are beneath our attention.

So it is with obscenities. Limited vocabulary results in the overuse of four-letter words, but there is strong and vital feeling in those words. Above all, the teacher should concentrate on the *communication*, rather than on what she has learned about "nice" words and "naughty" words. She might meditate, too, on the beautiful informality of using words without regard to their "morality." There is, after all, no "morality" in words. And the middle-class person who occasionally feels compelled to use an obscenity to express strong feeling is not as wise— or as comfortable—as he would be given the poor child's emphasis on communication rather than on disguising feelings with polite words.

No one is suggesting that teachers begin to use obscenities when speaking to poor children. Nor is the image of the middle-class, educated adult using the current slang particularly attractive. But there is a big difference between listening carefully to all words to understand meanings and to establish communication, and parroting the youngsters' language when one feels neither comfortable nor particularly communicative doing so.

The essential honesty of poor minority children enables them to detect dishonesty in teachers. They are sensitive to hypocritical protestations of tolerance and acceptance, and know very well when they are being rejected or denigrated, and why. They also recognize commitment to fair treatment, to *concern* for what happens to them and to honesty in human relationships.

Convinced of the honest commitment of a teacher, they can be as fiercely loyal and dedicated as they are to fellow gang members and to their own families. They will go so far as to "punish" recalcitrant pupils in the classroom, and "advise" the teacher to use physical force to maintain order. The teacher must be careful not to succumb to such "advice," or ever— even in desperation—to permit pupils to administer punishment. Children perpetuate the types of controls to which they are accustomed. It is the teacher's job to expose them to less violent means of control. Too often the teacher will accede to the cliché, "That's the only language they understand." It may very well be a "language" to which they have learned to respond. But this can never be justification for depriving them of the opportunity to learn other languages.

The creativity of poor minority youngsters is not limited to the invention of new words. At a recreation center recently I saw paintings done by children who had had a minimum of encouragement and opportunity. They were colorful, filled with feeling and with a form and style that no art teacher need feel ashamed of. I visited a school in which children from the most "deprived" homes were modelling in clay, with absorbed intensity, scenes which depicted the stories of their lives. The compositions they wrote, ungrammatical and limited in vocabulary as they were, showed a depth of feeling and a wealth of imagination that could lead any teacher to admiration and appreciation.

One teacher was moved to collect such creative, artistic expressions for a book he was "making." While the rest of the book described poverty, discouragement and hopelessness, in the children's own words, this part of the collection he labelled *The Beauty Part* in sincere, and somewhat surprised, appreciation.

Frank Reissman speaks of the amazing creativity of poor children in inventing games, since they rarely have the ready-made recreational facilities that middle-class children are surrounded by. With a blank wall, a piece of chalk and a ball, these children can invent fifteen or sixteen different games, each with intricate rules. What is more, they play their games with complete absorption—a clue, perhaps, to teaching them in the classroom.

Poor children, in general, are highly skeptical, even cynical. They have to be shown, in concrete and specific ways, what we want them to learn. Such skepticism, if we can help to make it somewhat selective and discriminating, can form the basis for really creative, individualistic functioning in a democratic society. How much more valuable in a democracy is the person who says "prove it!" than the one who is quick to be convinced by slogans, campaigns, rumors and promises! Poor children are pugnacious, quick to stand up for their rights and unafraid of change. But they will not be led to support any change at all just because articulate leaders call for it.

There is an egalitarianism in the societies of poor children and a refreshing informality which cuts through pose and pretense. People are evaluated by their behavior. Both of these attitudes embody our democratic ideals, and we would do well to encourage them in other segments of our society.

All these strengths of poor children should be seriously considered in evaluating the desegregated classroom. Too often, we perceive desegregation and integration as advantageous for the minority child alone. We overlook the very decided advantages to the majority child, to the middle- and upper-class child. (Or are we so afraid of informality, egalitarianism, pugnaciousness and skepticism that we regard them as weaknesses?)

Lack of Communication

Majority people are sometimes so intent on maintaining their own self-images as tolerant, accepting humanitarians that they cut themselves off from communication with and understanding of minority groups. Teachers fall into this trap too. Witness a public school Human Relations Committee discussing complaints from the parents of its few Mexican-American pupils that their children were treated differently than the other children. The parents felt that their children were dealt with more harshly, that physical punishment was used on them more often and that they were not given as much help with their lessons as other children received. When these feelings were reported to the Human Relations Committee by one or two articulate local residents, the Committee immediately set out to "change the image" of the school. Their solution to the problem was a circular, to be sent home with each child, assuring the parents that all children were given equal treatment!

Lack of communication with the dominant society and lack of recognition and respect dog the poor minority child throughout his life, resulting usually in failure in school and then failure as an adult. To fail again and again and again leads to an expectation of failure, a self-protective resistance to fighting it and a hopelessness about the future. The teacher must devote herself to recognizing and encouraging these children's strengths and successes, in whatever area. At first, these successes are unlikely to be in the subject matter area she teaches. But if she recognizes and applauds him, and helps the child and his classmates to value them, she may give children courage to work at mathematics and grammar.

10 Identifying Intergroup Problems in the Classroom

Raising Issues

Intergroup problems in the classroom are not difficult to identify if the teacher is willing to allow discussion of public events which involve issues of intergroup conflict. It does not always take a direct confrontation or investigation to reveal children's thoughts and feelings. But many teachers believe such disturbing subjects should be left unmentioned. When the 1964 World's Fair opened in New York, for example, one fifth-grade teacher in a midwestern city discussed at length the purposes of the Fair, and the exhibits and pavilions at the current fair and past fairs. She did not mention that men and women were picketing the site of the Fair in protest against employment discrimination or that others had announced their intention of blocking with their prostrate bodies the bridge approaches to the Fair. This teacher believed that such disturbing events were best withheld from her students because (a) they were too young to understand, (b) the class might get out of hand if they became embroiled in controversy, (c) the parents might object to discussions of such matters, (d) the administration might object to such discussions, and (e) the less talk there is about race relations, the less trouble there is between the races.

Another teacher in the same school did mention the demonstrators to her class. One of the children responded right away, "Those people had no right to block traffic." "They're colored," another child said, and a third grimaced and hunched his shoulders. The teacher learned a great deal about her students in the ensuing discussion which proved her colleague's assumptions unrealistic. The children already knew about the incident and had definite opinions about it. (They also displayed some misconceptions about the demonstration—white people as well as Negroes participated. They had strong feelings about Negro people, and some obvious discomfort at discussing the issue.)

But they were by no means innocent of all knowledge. Children, after all, watch television, read newspaper headlines, listen to adults and talk to each other. It would be difficult to identify a single subject they have never heard mentioned. And if we refuse to discuss certain subjects with them, we are leaving them to their own misinterpretations and misinformation.

In another city, violence erupted when a Negro family moved into an all-white neighborhood. Most of the teachers at the neighborhood junior high school agreed that the problem had no bearing on the school and preferred to "let sleeping dogs lie." But one teacher who was curious about his students' opinions of the harassment of the Negro family, the rock-throwing at the police, and the confident announcement by a Ku Klux Klan leader that he would organize the whites in the community, asked them one day, "What is it all about?" The observations came out in a rush. "Those niggers just want to cause trouble. They get paid to." "Colored always want to live with white." "Why do they go where they're not wanted? I never would." "We have the right to have our own neighborhood." These children, who lived in an all-white neighborhood, knew no Negroes and had not met the new Negro family, were confident they knew all about Negroes. Yet they knew nothing about the pressures which drive Negro families to move into neighborhoods where they are not wanted or about the rights guaranteed by our legal system. Even a teacher who believes his responsibilities limited to teaching facts must agree that these children's factual misinformation should have been corrected. But even a conservative definition of the classroom teacher's function involves teaching children to evaluate information thoughtfully and to draw reasonable conclusions from available facts.

Inasmuch as intergroup relations problems are intellectual ones requiring intellectual solutions, the teacher needs no more justification for helping her students solve them than she does to help them with mathematics problems. If it is the function of the teacher to help students define reality and deal with it adequately, then the facts, ideas and processes of human interaction constitute legitimate curricular offerings.

It is easy to see, too, that unsolved intergroup problems are often directly related to low aspirations, low achievement and discipline difficulties, all surely within the province of the classroom teacher. But in intergroup relations more than in other subjects, the teacher cannot expect optimum achievement if she relies only on "telling" in her teaching. She must also, gradually at first if she finds it very difficult, leave time to listen to her students. Children need opportunities to talk out their intergroup feelings and beliefs, and the teacher must listen if she is to know what her pupils need from her.

Talking, asking questions, rewording answers and testing ideas on others are important in all learning, and they are a vital first step in changing emotionally-toned attitudes. The mere admission of hostility is salutary, for without it feelings of antagonism cannot be honestly examined. If children feel free to express themselves, they may eventually learn how to respond to different attitudes, to test the effects of attitudes on different individuals and to relate attitudes to behavior. All of this must go on in an atmosphere of safety, where hostility is not punished but is examined for purposes of understanding.

Encouraging Discussion

In the multi-group classroom, the teacher may find majority-group children reluctant to discuss intergroup problems. They may tell her privately that they would prefer not to talk about "race," because they do not want to hurt the feelings of the minority-group children. It is easy to view such sentiments as evidence of sensitivity and good will, and far too easy to abandon discussion of intergroup problems at this "clear evidence" that the children have no such problems! But let us examine this sentiment more carefully, by asking what there is in the attitudes of the majority children which would hurt the feelings of minority children if expressed aloud. Do the majority-group children really know anything about the attitudes and feelings of minority children? (If they have never talked to each other about these things, how could they know?) The teacher must also ask herself why she is tempted to accede to the children's requests not to discuss intergroup problems.

Minority-group children may display a similar reluctance to discuss intergroup problems. They, too, may not want to disrupt the surface harmony of their daily relationships with their classmates. But the fundamental question here is whether growth in mutual understanding and the elimination of traditional barriers to free communication are worth some initial discomfort at the introduction of emotionally-toned subjects.

It often happens, when the uncomfortable question is raised in class, that the children of only one group participate in the discussion. Or, perhaps, two or three brave little souls do all the talking while the others sit in awkward silence. The discomfort the children feel may be almost palpable; it is evidence of habitual avoidance of the subject, lack of experience in talking about the subject, feelings of guilt at hostility felt but not expressed, and fear that their hostility will become apparent. All these feelings are real and strong, and they can interfere with communication, with learning and with health. If they are not dealt with realistically, the child can be permanently handicapped.

After their initial reticence disappears, the children may tend to agree or disagree along group lines, whether the subject is intergroup relations, the war in Vietnam or the quality of the food in the lunchroom. It is easy to attribute such opinion splits to basic cultural differences between groups, and in many instances this diagnosis is correct. One major purpose of discussing intergroup problems in the classroom is, of course, to diminish the isolation which causes such differences of outlook. As discussion continues, this kind of polarization gradually declines. (The teacher should be aware of the possibility that one group may, by virtue of its life experiences, have information not available to the other group. Direct and indirect experience with employment discrimination is not unusual among minority children, for example, while majority children in the same city may be completely unaware of the existence of discrimination.)

There would seem to be two possible responses to the discomfort most people feel in talking about intergroup problems. The teacher may see evidence that some of the children are withdrawing, physically or psychologically, during the discussion. The child who moves his chair out of the circle or turns in his seat to face away from the other children, is trying to remove himself physically from the situation. It is not so easy to detect the child who has removed himself psychologically. Indications may be as subtle as a demeanor of sincere and attentive absorption, (though the eyes are somewhat fixed) or as blatant as throwing a book at another student.

It is pretty clear that intergroup problems cannot be solved by avoidance. The old idea that "time" will, in some mysterious way, eliminate problems is simply not realistic. Time removes people, but not before they have perpetuated the problem by transmitting their fears, hostilities and misconceptions to their children. The alternative to avoidance is to recognize our discomfort and to talk about it, trying to understand what it is that is making us uncomfortable, and getting help in understanding from others. In the process, we struggle with new concepts, share each other's experiences and try to feel what others feel. Gradually, the discomfort is dissipated, and we are eventually so comfortable with the subject that it surprises us to encounter people who are reluctant to talk about intergroup relations.

Observing Behavior

In apparently harmonious multi-group schools, it is relatively easy to determine whether children are having difficulty relating to each other across group lines. If the children eat lunch at school, you may observe Negro children sitting at one table and white children at another. If the students eat in neighborhood sandwich shops, it may be customary for Spanish-speaking children to congregate in a shop which is never patronized by the other students. In elementary schools where the children go home for lunch, separation along group lines may be observed in the school yard. The children may play only with members of their own groups, crossing group lines only to argue or to fight. Whatever the immediate reasons for these voluntary separations, they are symptomatic. To assume that the attitudes they represent are not destructive is unwarranted without careful examination. They may indicate predispositions to fight and to denigrate.

Most people do not go where they are not wanted. (The few hardy individuals who bravely buck the exclusion out of conviction or desperate necessity attract much attention but remain few in number.) The results of this natural reluctance are evident in the pattern of extracurricular participation in desegregated schools. There are certain offices and clubs, usually the most prestigious, which minority-group youngsters simply do not bother to apply for. It is easy to conclude that they are not interested, and easy to insist that a particular activity has no minority-group members because none apply. But let us investigate a little more closely. In one Eastern high school, both Negroes and whites assured a visitor that they had no intergroup problems. The visitor acknowledged their opinions and waited for further comment. "Well," one Negro youngster said hesitantly, "colored can't join the sculling club." A white student hastened to explain, "It's nobody's fault in the school. It's just that colored aren't allowed on the river." The sculling club was a prestige activity, and Negro students felt unjustly excluded from it. White students salved their consciences, when the subject occurred to them, by shifting the blame to some imaginary public ordinance. And nobody had ever discussed the issue in the twenty-five years of the club's existence!

A similar situation came to light in a southwestern junior high school, where certain desirable clubs had no Spanish students. The advisor to the ceramics club, the most popular in the school, at first denied that her group had never had a Spanish member. When presented with irrefutable evidence, she maintained that Spanish children never applied. Asked whether she thought Spanish children, by virtue of their ethnic background, had no interest in ceramics, the teacher burst out with an emotional defense of her right to choose the club's members because she paid for most of the materials out of her own pocket!

Sociometry

Even individuals who resist encouragement to talk openly or who attempt to withdraw from class discussions reveal their feelings in ways a sensitive teacher can decipher. Hostile looks, *sotto voce* insults, and perpetual feuds which seem to be constantly refueled can say a great deal. Also, simple sociometric techniques can help the teacher diagnose patterns of association in the classroom objectively and systematically. Questions like, "Whom would you like to sit next to on the bus when we take our trip?" and "Which three people would you like to work with on your committee?" administered in written form, accurately reveal the degree of separation along group lines. If children repeatedly make the same choices for both classroom and extracurricular projects, we may conclude that personal attractiveness and habitual association are their only criteria for choices of companions, and that they need help in recognizing the importance of other attributes.

Once she has identified the criteria on which students make their choices of friends, the teacher may use her information to change the pattern of interaction. Cooperative work groups are an excellent setting for encouraging children to work together across group lines. But if competition is the predominant philosophy of the class, voluntary choice of work groups will probably reinforce ethnic cleavages. Instead, the teacher may arrange groupings to encourage the students to make contact with new people. She may do this by giving the isolated children, and those who are rarely chosen by others, first choice of work groups. She may assign an unaccepted person to work with friendly, helpful students, or a shy rejected student to the same group with a friendly protective child. In the process of working together toward a common goal, students who have not really recognized each other's existence may suddenly "see" the other person as someone of value.

In the event of intergroup hostility or avoidance, the teacher may raise the question of why one's best friend is not always the person best equipped to help a group complete a particular task. The children can prove for themselves that the articulate Negro girl may be a wiser choice for group spokesman than the shy but popular white girl. The Indian boy interested in airplanes may be a better choice for a transportation project than the white boy who is the class football star.

Of course such associations may prove disastrous if students are so blinded by their antipathies and resentments that they cannot work together. Here the teacher must help them to understand what it is they are resisting and to recognize how they themselves suffer if they continue to limit their associations to their close friends and their "own kind."

In everyday decision-making, the relevant differences between people are functional ones. If John Jones does not want the Student Council to meet on Tuesday because he must work after school that day, and Bob Smith prefers Tuesdays because it gets him out of cleaning the furnace, the fact that John Jones is Negro and Bob Smith white is irrelevant. But these facts become very relevant if the students examine the qualifications

for Council membership and begin to suspect that the requirements which invariably eliminate Negroes from membership
exist for just that purpose.

Analyzing the Fights

Overt conflict between children of different groups should be
investigated very carefully for evidence of intergroup conflict.
Intergroup fights are often explained away as "normal" conflict
between two individuals with no racial significance. Examination of the situation will often reveal, however, that racial
factors precipitated or intensified the conflict. If two children
are fighting over a ball and one calls the other a "black nigger,"
we must ask ourselves why, from among all the possible insults
available to this child, he chose a racial epithet. A child may
need to be helped to understand why he does not respond with
overt hostility when white Johnny demonstrates annoying behavior, but does when brown Johnny acts in exactly the same
way. Children may actually perceive brown Johnny's behavior
as different from white Johnny's. How to make them realize
that they often see and feel what they want and expect to see?

One technique involves the use of readily-available materials. Pictures from magazines and newspapers that the children have not seen before can be used to demonstrate to them
that people with different attitudes actually see the world differently. Show them a picture with Oriental and Occidental
people in it, and ask each child to interpret the situation it
depicts. The children's interpretations will reflect their own
experiences, fears, prejudices, antagonisms and preferences.
Ask them to do the same with an incident that has just occurred
in the schoolyard or the lunchroom: let them compare their
various interpretations of the same situation. Help them to
look for the sources of their different points of view in their
own lives. Ask them what they mean when they call someone
a wop or a greaser. Ask minority children how they feel about
those words. Do the words mean only "I am angry with you?"
Or do they also mean "You are inferior to me," and "Your
kind are all alike."? The confusion surrounding the facts about
groups and individuals is revealed when the children separate
their feelings and beliefs from the available facts. No one is
better equipped than the teacher to help them see the difference between opinion and fact. After a while, they may stop

laughing at facile generalizations, like "That's a man for you!" or, "Women drivers!" They may realize the serious difficulties in human relationships that result from the kind of generalizing that pictures human beings, not as they really are, but through a haze of stereotype.

Often, interracial conflict which occurs outside the classroom is considered to be beyond the province of the classroom teacher. Administrators are fond of saying, "We have no intergroup problems in school. They all exist outside—on the way home, in the community, in the neighborhood." This is analogous to saying that we have no crimes because none are committed in the presence of policemen. Nevertheless, wherever they erupt, the problems are the children's. If the community situation is such that the children's problems are not being solved, the school is the logical agency to undertake the job. In the teaching of social studies, we should not be concerned merely with the rote memorization of lists of dates and historical events. Facts that are memorized and never used are soon forgotten. If social studies does not deal with the problems of everyday living, what of lasting value does the child learn in the social studies class?

If fighting is a problem in the neighborhood, the fight may be reenacted in the safe climate of the classroom. In the process of taking first one side and then another and observing the effects of feelings and behavior on the course of events, the children may discover alternatives to fighting. If children have few words and experiences to draw on, their solutions to problems tend to be rigid and violent. If they see the choices and discuss them, their solutions may be more constructive and more conducive to harmonious human relationships.

Recognizing Feelings

As we have noted before, we must not overlook the intergroup ramifications of a fight between two Negro children, in which one calls the other a "nigger." The general American acceptance of "white" as a pervasive value—white skin, white lies, white purity—may cause serious conflict in the American Negro child. If, in the United States, white is good and black is bad, if white is pure and black is sin, how does a black child feel about his own color? If he rejects his own blackness, because as an American he believes white to be superior, he is in trouble. How can a human being function adequately with this kind of self-hatred? It is something in the nature of a miracle that most minority-group people in our society live adequate lives!

In one all-Negro class, a Negro teacher prepared to read her sixth-graders a story. "This," he began, "is the story of a black child." More than a few of the children snickered and giggled at the announcement. Why? What discomfort did they feel at public acknowledgment of their color? Why are they discomfited? Why don't they hear with calm acceptance that they are black? How many white children would have their equilibrium shaken by a suggestion that they were to hear a story about a white child? (At most, they might wonder why it was necessary to mention it at all. Aren't all stories about white children? But in the world of most black children, few stories are about blacks.)

"I don't like colored," the white six-year-old says, and actually shudders with the intensity of her fear. "Indians are lazy," says the teen-age sophisticate, reassuring himself that, no matter what his father says, there are people who are lazier than he is. "You can't trust a Mex," says the twelve-year-old solemnly, parodying his uncle's bravado, "They'll knife you as soon as look at you."

Overt expressions of prejudice are obvious indications of attitudes and feelings about racial, religious and nationality groups. Yet here too the timid adult may be quick to smooth over the implications of such expressions. "Oh, he didn't mean anything by it." Or, "They're just children. They don't know what they're saying." Though it is true children often do not know what they are saying, they most certainly *feel* what they are saying, and they need help in understanding those feelings and developing more accepting ones.

An Evaluation Checklist

Some time ago, I developed a checklist for teachers and school administrators to use in evaluating the intergroup situation in their own schools.[1] Many of them have found the checklist

[1] Adapted from "Evaluating Intergroup Relations Education," *The Bulletin of the National Association of Secondary School Principals*, 44: 174–179 (October, 1960), by permission of the National Association of Secondary School Principals, 1960. Copyright: Washington, D.C.

useful as a diagnostic tool, and a guide in designing curricular and extracurricular activities to improve intergroup relations. Though originally developed with the secondary school in mind, there is no reason why it cannot be used successfully in elementary schools.

The checklist is based on three principles on which an effective intergroup relations program must be built.

Part I raises general questions about the efforts being made in the school to explore and solve intergroup problems. The questions assume a recognition by school administrators of the need for such exploration.

The questions in Part II point out specific behaviors that reveal the degree and kind of intergroup conflict in the school and community. The assumption is made that school and community are inseparable, and that community problems and activities are reflected in the relationships in the school.

Part III concentrates on the efforts of faculty and administration to enable all the people involved in the school to improve their relationships with each other.

An adequate educational program should deal with three aspects of intergroup relations:

1. Young people need facts about groups other than their own and about how groups interact with each other in various social settings.

2. Young people need an awareness of and sensitivity to the needs and problems of groups other than their own.

3. Young people need ample opportunity to develop skills in interacting creatively with people of groups other than their own.

I. General Nature and Organization of the Program

    A. General Nature of the Program

        1. Is there an organized, on-going attempt to identify, analyze, and solve intergroup relations problems? (Is there, for example, a program of social attitude testing?)

        2. Is there adequate minority-group representation on all committees and clubs working on intergroup problems? (Adequate minority-group representa-

tion involves not only numbers but representatives who are friendly but firm in their attempts to improve minority-group conditions, and who are not afraid or reluctant to take a stand in mixed-group organizations.)

3. Are outside professionals in intergroup relations an integral part of in-service intergroup relations education?

4. Is there an on-going program designed to explore and develop methods of inducing the best-qualified teachers to remain? (This is particularly important in schools with a changing population or a lower socio-economic population.)

B. Organization of the Program

1. Is there a continuous formal program in intergroup relations education for teachers and administrators?

2. Are there special units on intergroup relations in required social studies courses? (Or a required course in intergroup relations?)

3. Have the teachers who teach intergroup relations had formal education in this field?

4. Does the school have a faculty-administration-student intergroup relations committee which meets regularly?

5. Is there some kind of intergroup relations club in the co-curriculum program?

II. *Evaluation of Intergroup Relations in the School*

A. Among Students

1. At lunch time and other non-directed periods, do Negro and white students, Christian and Jewish students, Catholic and Protestant students, and students of different nationality groups mix in their seating and associations?

2. Are some clubs in the co-curriculum program consistently made up of a single racial, religious or nationality group?

3. Is any group (or groups) consistently excluded from some clubs?

4. Does any group (or groups) consistently avoid applying for membership in some clubs?
5. What are students' attitudes (determined by a program of attitude testing) toward racial, religious, and nationality groups other than their own?
6. How do minority students feel about their opportunities for participation in the co-curriculum program?
7. How do minority students feel about the fairness of teachers?
8. How do minority students feel about their acceptance by other students?
9. Is there any overt evidence of intergroup tension among students?
   a. Do students use racial or other group epithets when they are in conflict?
   b. Are there formal or informal gangs or cliques among students made up along group lines?
   c. Are there rumors of actual or potential violence between groups?
   d. Is there evidence of fear of any racial, religious, or nationality group among other students?
   e. Is there a pattern of mischief by one group or against one group?
   f. Are there intergroup fights among students outside of school?

B. Among Faculty and Administration Members
   1. Is there a larger than normal turnover of experienced faculty members?
   2. If the school is considered difficult to teach in, is the average length of experience of faculty members greater than normal?
   3. Are different racial and religious groups represented on the faculty?
   4. Are there signs of friction along group lines among faculty members?
   5. Do faculty members regularly discuss school problems in intergroup relations, including intra-faculty problems?

6. Is the administration committed to a schoolwide program in intergroup relations?

C. In the Community

    1. Is the community a segregated one; *i.e.,* is it made up of only one group or of a number of isolated groups?

    2. What are the employment problems of minority-group people in the community?

    3. Is there intergroup tension in the community? (In one-group communities, this may take the form of fear that a minority-group will come in, resentment by a minority group that its housing is limited to this community, lack of sensitivity to current intergroup problems, refusal to discuss intergroup problems, *etc.*)

    4. Are there agencies in the community working to improve intergroup relations?

III. *Methods of Ameliorating Intergroup Relations*

    A. Teaching Method

        1. Do students have opportunities to learn democratic skills and values by interacting in problem-solving groups?

        2. Are the problem-solving groups concerned with real problems in intergroup relations which are of immediate relevance to the lives of the students?

        3. Are role-playing, feedback, analysis of group roles, sociometry, and other techniques used to help students understand both themselves and the dynamics of group interaction?

        4. Do students have opportunities to meet and work with people of many ethnic and social groups?

    B. Encouraging Involvement

        1. Does the administration actively participate in and encourage faculty participation in community intergroup problems?

        2. Does the administration provide time and facilities for faculty study of the community from which the students are drawn?

3. Are community members—including the parents of students—invited individually or in small groups to meet teachers, administrators and students, observe classes, discuss problems and in other ways to become active participants in the life of the school? (In addition to the parent-teacher association, which often appears to operate tangentially to the school rather than in it.)

4. Do the administrators *and faculty members* have regular opportunities to meet with the administrators and faculties of other schools to compare experiences?

11 Solving Intergroup Problems in the Classroom

Taking the Initiative

When the teacher sees a pattern of exclusion among her students, that is, that minority-group youngsters are ignored socially, excluded from the most desirable activities or isolated during lunch, she has a choice to make. She can help students become aware of their unconscious attitudes and behavior, or she can avoid the problem. She can take the initiative in breaking the pattern, or she can say, "You can't force integration," or "It's natural for people to want to be with their friends," or "Indians prefer to be with their own kind."

Often the teacher need only raise the issue, and students will take it up out of curiosity about a phenomenon they have not previously noticed. Some few may even decide to break the pattern of voluntary segregation by sitting with another group during lunch, chatting with the other group before and after class or sitting near a member of another group in class.

Most teachers know that teaching by example is more meaningful than teaching by precept. The teacher who begins to eat in the student lunchroom, and to encourage members of minority and majority groups to join her, can act as a catalyst for changing patterns of association. (In the process, too, she may learn something about herself: how she feels about associating with youngsters outside the classroom, how she feels about eating with people of another race or why she has never taken it upon herself before to break down a pattern of segregation.)

One area in which teacher initiative can be especially productive is in extracurricular activities. Club advisors are generally very influential with youngsters, and raising the question with club leaders of why there are no minority students in a particular club, or why no minority students run for office, may result in conscious efforts to let minority students know that they are wanted and to encourage them to join. Putting the qualifications for club membership *in writing* helps make clear to all students that there is no tacit exclusion of any group. It does not hurt to say in so many words that no one is excluded because of race, religion or national origin. Sometimes, teachers and administrators are reluctant to write such a statement. They feel that it implies that there has been group discrimination in the past, and that it is only now being discontinued. Others feel that making such a statement encourages youngsters to discriminate when they would never have thought of it by themselves. Both objections help us to avoid solving existing problems. Prejudice and discrimination are pervasive facts in our society, and we often must dissociate ourselves from them openly if we are to convince both perpetrators and victims that we are determined to be fair to everyone.

Role-Playing

One of the most effective methods of expressing attitudes and observing behavior in an atmosphere of safety is role-playing. Many teachers use a form of role-playing, though they usually do not call it by name. Children studying history often pretend to be historical figures and act out significant events. In an attempt to help children understand a particular situation or relationship in their own lives, a teacher may say to a child, "Now, pretend I am your mother and explain to me why your teacher is keeping you after school today." All of us have watched children pretending to be adults and playing "house" or "school." What they are doing is taking the parts of other people and trying to understand how those people feel and think. They are trying for a period to do what they believe those other people would do. There is much to be learned from putting yourself in someone else's shoes, experiencing something from his vantage point and making the effort to understand his motivations and to feel what he is feeling.

When several individuals take turns at the same role, it becomes clear that perceptions of other people vary. Role-players must then try to learn the sources of differential perception. In the process, they learn much about themselves—

why they think and feel about some things the way they do.

Also, different ways of playing the same role elicit different responses from the other protagonists in the scene, and the whole course of events in an incident may be changed when one role-player changes his interpretation of the role.

Such a learning situation is not threatening to children because insults, hostilities, anger and misconceptions are all expressed by "pretend" characters. The person playing the part cannot be held responsible—and hence punished—for such expressions. Thus while the child is learning about how it feels to be someone else, and looking at his own behavior, he is safe from retaliatory recriminations for his errors.

The teacher can use this method specifically to develop intergroup understanding. A white child may take the role of a Negro child in a playground scene and learn something about how it feels to be excluded. A Negro child may take the role of a white child and reveal in his behavior his own feelings about the hostility and arrogance of white people. During role-playing, children may object safely to a pretend-teacher's discriminatory behavior. (And the real teacher may see the need to modify her own behavior!) Children may use role-playing to test alternative solutions to problems and examine the effects of each one before deciding on the most efficacious method. This kind of experimenting with solutions involves establishing criteria for the ways people are treated. The values implicit in behavior are examined for fairness and rationality. In the process of testing alternative behaviors, new values are suggested, and students may find support from each other in accepting those new values and the new forms of behavior they suggest.

Role-playing may often serve to overcome the initial difficulty of speaking directly to intergroup problems. Though a white child may feel too uncomfortable to admit that he is afraid of Negroes, he may be able to take the role of another white child and demonstrate his fear by saying, in effect, "Other people, not I, are afraid of Negroes." As the class tries to understand people's fears of each other, they may develop some ease in discussing the subject and eventually find the courage to admit their own fears. There is no shortcut to, or substitute for, speaking candidly about one's feelings and beliefs, if we are to develop self-insight, understanding and acceptance of ourselves and of others.

Cooperative Teaching

Many teachers who recognize the importance of intergroup education feel unable, emotionally and intellectually, to accept the responsibility for teaching the subject. There are ways for such a teacher to help herself. She may find it easier to approach the subject if she has some support from others. It is not difficult, logistically, to cooperate with a friend-colleague and teach as a team. In this way two teachers can support each other emotionally, cooperate in planning and searching for material and discuss with each other the problems that arise and the progress they are making. Sometimes, to ease into the subject less painfully, the teacher may call on intergroup workers in the community to present their views and encourage the pupils to speak. In almost every area in the country, there are intergroup workers attached to intergroup agencies, settlement houses, churches, universities and community centers who would be pleased to visit a classroom to help the teacher teach intergroup relations. Most of these workers know the intergroup problems of the community, and if they do not have the advantage of the teacher's knowledge and skill in education, they can at least supply the intergroup facts that teachers and pupils may need.

Because most schools in the United States are still essentially one-group schools, with minimal or token minority representation, the child in the one-group classroom has little opportunity to interact with children of other groups and thus develop skill in intergroup relationships. The teacher who wants to fill this gap in his children's learning may arrange with an interested teacher in a one-group minority school for joint sessions for the two classes. This requires considerable planning and some legwork. A mere visit from one class to another is of questionable value. The real value in making contact across group lines lies in identifying common problems, learning each others' feelings and beliefs and working on common tasks. If this is a startlingly new idea in your school, it might be a good idea to find a colleague who would like to undertake a similar project for her class. If two teachers in a school plan for such an activity, they receive comfort and support from each other.

Some city school systems, recognizing the intergroup needs of teachers, are developing in-service programs to further teacher education in this area. These programs are designed to inform, to provoke discussion and to initiate action. Philadelphia, for example, has hired an intergroup relations staff to encourage intergroup programming in all schools. It has also developed a series of television programs for school personnel. After each program, the school people divide into small groups to discuss what they have seen and how it applies to their own situations. The Massachusetts State Department of Education has developed an excellent television series in intergroup relations, with recognized experts in the field exchanging ideas with working school people. New York City's Operation Understanding sends teachers to Puerto Rican schools and assigns Puerto Rican teachers to New York schools, in the hope that returning teachers can contribute to increased understanding between Puerto Ricans and mainlanders.

Temple University in Philadelphia offers courses in Intergroup Relations and Intergroup Education for local teachers, arranges lectures to which school people are invited and releases faculty members for participation in school intergroup programs. Even a project like the Teacher Corps, a unit of which is being trained at Temple University and in the Philadelphia and Trenton, New Jersey school systems, is a source of intergroup education for in-service teachers. Teacher Corpsmen, participating actively in the solution of community problems and getting help and guidance from the University, are helping other teachers in their schools to proceed along similar lines.

Organizations like the Urban League and the National Conference of Christians and Jews, branches of which are found in most regions of the country, offer seminars, workshops and speakers to help teachers learn more about intergroup problems. Businessmen and other workers in the community can also offer something to the cooperative education venture. They can visit the classroom to talk with the children about the work they do and how they prepared for it. Minority children ought to be exposed to people and situations which will convince them that they can succeed just as others have.

Majority children usually have these success models at home and in their communities but they do not know successful minority people, a gap which visits from minority businessmen can fill. Poor children, especially poor minority children, generally do not have such models unless the teacher provides them. Successful members of their own group, as well as business owners who assert their policy of hiring on merit, can do much to encourage them.

Exploding the Myth of Homogeneity

So-called homogeneous grouping probably does more to impede the development of good intergroup relations than any other social concept. In our society, we are assured that people would "rather be with their own kind." We conveniently overlook the strivings of people to mingle socially and vocationally, the endless attempts of minority people to become part of the mainstream of American life and the millions of majority people who travel, move and change jobs, endlessly adjusting to new groups and new situations. We also overlook the fact that it is often fear that makes us stick with "our own kind." It is important to eliminate such fear, rather than accept its results as natural and inevitable.

In the classroom, the myth of homogeneous grouping is perpetuated. We teachers know that each child is different and that, though we may lessen the range of ability in a group, we will never have a group of children with identical ability, the same learning style or the same responses to frustration. But some people delude themselves by labelling a group homogeneous in order to justify teaching many children the same thing at the same time in the same way and assuming that they are learning.

It is more realistic to group together a child who reads easily, another who has considerable difficulty in learning to read, one who reads indifferently but draws beautifully, one who is kind and helpful and another who is frightened and timid. These children can all learn from each other and help each other and can, with support and advice from the teacher, supplement her efforts to teach them. There is evidence that even poor readers increase their level of achievement in the process of helping those less able than themselves. Children of varying skills, gathered together for a common goal and interested in the steps leading to that goal, can become really involved in the learning process. Few children who sit passively in a class listening to the teacher talk are as intellectually and emotionally active.

There are times when the teacher may want to speak for a few moments to all of the children at once, or ask them all to practice something as a group. There are other times when she may want to work with one group, or with two groups together. She may invite a specialist from the community or a teaching colleague to give some special assistance to one or more groups, or she may ask a child from one group to help the members of another group. She may go home with a child at the end of the day to show his mother how to help him develop a particular skill, or she may take five or six children to a bottling plant to help them visualize some of the things they have been reading about automation. Such activities illustrate the flexibility that begins to characterize the learning-teaching process when we escape the rigidity of the "homogeneous" classroom.

The significance of the whole question of ability grouping for human relations lies partly in the effects of separation on attitudes. There is evidence that high-achievers who are isolated from low achievers begin to think of themselves as superior human beings, instead of just better readers or spellers. They begin to think that they should not associate with the "low" group. They cannot see that there is more to a person than just the ability to get a good grade in school. If communication between achievement levels is cut off, people lose sight of the universal human goals we all share. In addition, the idea is perpetuated that those who do not achieve *cannot* achieve; the feeling persists that all disabilities are innate. Our failure to discover more efficient ways of teaching is sanctioned when the burden of failure is transferred from us to the child, who is, in reality, the victim.

Seeing Discipline Problems as Internal Disharmony

We teachers and principals often concentrate on external order in an attempt to achieve something called discipline. We ignore the fact that the externally imposed order of the traditional classroom may mask internal disharmony, which interferes with learning and frequently erupts despite the teacher's restraining influence. What are the elements of this disharmony, especially those related to intergroup relations, and what can the classroom teacher do about them?

Children do not live their lives in the classroom. They live in a world where Negroes, Indians, Mexican-Americans and Puerto Ricans are rejected. Whether through the subtle snub, casual derogation or rocks thrown at the window of a home, minority groups are told they are inferior, unwanted and less than human. This results in, among other things, an unrealistic self-image: white children think they are somehow superior just because they are white; minority children have doubts about their own worth just because they are members of minorities. Insofar as people's choices are influenced by these errors, there can be no harmony between them and their environment or between them and other human beings. For example, a white person who does not achieve success may look for the causes of his failure not within himself, but in the increasing opportunity for Negro people. And a Negro child may not even try to succeed because he is convinced it is useless.

It is the teacher's responsibility, not to ignore the inconsistencies in our lives, but to help children see them for what they are: the inadequacies of human beings. The minority child who will not try because he is sure he will fail, needs patient encouragement to try for the things he wants. He must at every step of the way see the relationship between school tasks and satisfaction of his life's needs. He needs to be taught how to take a hand in his own destiny rather than be destroyed by the needs of others.

The majority child needs to look within himself for his own worth, not to find it by denigrating others. He, too, needs praise and encouragement; he, too, must see the relevance of school to his total life.

The student can develop a sense of self-worth in a number of ways: praise, awareness that the teacher accepts his feelings and ideas without criticism; and recognition that she is interested in him and wants to hear what he has to say. An understanding of the past is important too. (For example, a teacher with a true knowledge of the significance of Negroes in American and world history does not relegate Negro Americans to an annual Negro History week, but sees Negroes sharing the agonies of a developing nation with other Americans, often victimized but growing remarkably in pride and strength despite massive obstacles. An accurate picture of American history helps young Negroes to see themselves as people of worth, with a heritage of courage. It helps young whites to see themselves realistically as only one kind of American and one shade of human beings, *all* of whom have their share of successes and failures.)

The teacher would do well to learn something about her students outside of the classroom. Teachers of poor children are often amazed at the level of aspiration, articulateness and the creativity of children who in the classroom are dull or troublesome. Full knowledge of her children's capacities and of what they really want out of life can help the teacher to make American history and elementary science, spelling and Shakespeare relevant to her pupils, and interest them in their own education. If the teacher demonstrates that she thinks the students are worth knowing, she may convince them that they are worthwhile.

Adding to childrens' confusion about what is expected of them—a confusion we often call "lack of discipline"—is the democratic philosophy preached in textbooks, a philosophy that we do not really live by. The neat precepts about every man being equal just do not seem applicable to the minority child's life in America. But neither do they mean anything in the school life of the majority child. Are children in school really part of a democratic society? The chances are that we adults are too intent on providing children what we think they need to concern ourselves with what *they* think they need.

Many teachers are finding a way to mitigate the effects of unrealistic texts and, at the same time, to give children an exciting experience in self-expression. Instead of relying exclusively on text books, they are letting their children, even the lowest achievers among them, write their own books. The content of these books is drawn from their own experiences in and outside the classroom. The joy of success children feel when they find they can *read* their books simply cannot be described! One group of Negro third-graders wrote a book about friends: "Friends like you. Friends sometimes fight. I take a walk with my friends." These observations arose out of classroom discussions, and each child was helped to write down his own observations. Then the children illustrated the pages, writing the "captions" at the bottom of the drawings. When all the material was organized into a *Friendship Book,* they began to cast their sights outside the classroom for new friends with whom to share the book. It was arranged for them to spend a day with a class of Puerto Rican children in another school. It was not long before they were adding new pages to the book, with captions about friends who spoke another language, who knew about foods you had never experienced and who were different but also in many ways the same.

Disseminating Facts

The classroom teacher has a unique opportunity, in her role as a disseminator of facts, to improve intergroup relations. No matter which subject she teaches, no matter what her teaching style or personality, she can weave into the content of her courses facts about race, about ethnic groups and about group interaction. Locomotives, whose speeds are to be computed, may be carrying Chinese workers to work on American railroads. Farm products of the northeastern United States may be harvested by migrant workers from the south or from Puerto Rico. And problems can be designed dealing with the number of minority people in a city, the number of new houses available, housing discrimination and the resultant number of minority people who can afford new homes but must live in substandard ghetto housing. There is no subject that does not have a human component and thus no subject that does not lend itself to intergroup education. Part IV is devoted to illustrating the possibilities of this approach in several subject matter areas.

12 Classroom Discipline and Controversial Subjects

Good Noise

Recently 648 elementary school teachers were polled on whether they dealt with controversial issues in their social studies programs.[1] Eighty per cent of them said they did not. Only eleven per cent felt they were competent to handle such issues in the classroom, and one common explanation for their reluctance was that, "The children quickly get out of hand when we discuss something unusual like that." This concern with classroom discipline is pervasive among teachers and is, I think, the most important single influence on the method and content of teaching.

To many people, discipline means silence. Again and again, teaching interns are reprimanded when the principal looks into a classroom and finds the children talking and moving around the room. Student teachers are commended, "When I went past your room this afternoon, I thought an experienced teacher was conducting the class; it was so quiet."

Occasionally a secure and courageous intern, reprimanded for a noisy class, will protest, "But that's *good* noise. The children are all involved and interested. They're planning and working together." The traditional answer is simply, "No noise is good noise."

Rule-Book Etiquette

We assume that it is necessary for a group of adults working out a problem to talk to each other. But if we believe that children learn best by listening attentively to what the teacher tells them, there is indeed no reason for more than one person to make a sound. Everything we know about individual learning styles, the need for continuous feedback to check children's

[1] J. D. McAulay, "Controversial Issues in the Social Studies," *Education*, 86:27–30 (September, 1965).

understanding of a lesson and the desirability of active participation in the learning process, is ignored. Instead, we hark
back to the rules of politeness. Archaic precepts like, "Children do not speak unless spoken to," and the universally un-
learned exhortation, "Do not speak when someone else is
speaking" are, to say the least, tangential to our professional
goals. There is an implication in these rules that observing
them denotes respect for the person speaking. By extension,
the child-noise in a room where the teacher does most of the
talking becomes a mark of disrespect—for the teacher, for
authority and for school. Such "disrespect" is, in classroom
terms, a discipline problem. Thus, the activity of the children,
and the relationship between children and teacher, are not
analyzed for the identification and solution of the multitude
of educational problems they embody. Instead, they are viewed
as simply right or wrong, and either wholly approved or wholly
disapproved. (Incidentally, how quiet are we teachers, even at
a lecture we attend voluntarily? I think there are few adult
groups as "noisy" as professional educators at a lecture!)

Emotional Expression

Too often, we teachers are afraid to hear emotions expressed.
We have visions of anger exploding into physical attacks. At
the very least, we envision a complete loss of class control,
resulting in chaos. Actually, the study of human behavior
teaches us that those who can satisfactorily express their anger
verbally will not need to attack physically; it is usually children
of few words who confront every conflict situation by fighting.
Such children even seek opportunities to fight because they
cannot put into words their inner conflicts and frustrations.
The children who can express their anger safely, without fear
of reprimand or punishment, and then proceed to examine the
sources of their anger, are far less likely to hit each other.

Teachers who pride themselves on the quiet "well-behaved"
children in their classes are often forcing the children to bottle
up strong feelings. Priding themselves on the good discipline
in their classrooms, teachers ignore or are unaware of the havoc
being caused, either inside the child or between children on
the way home from school.

The teacher who does have difficulty with discipline fears
that discussion of an emotionally-toned subject will cost her

the little control she has. Actually, if the children can concentrate on expressing their feelings about a particular subject, they will not need to fidget, annoy each other, wander around the room and, finally, in desperation, hit someone.

If children are involved in a heated discussion, they may not always wait for permission to speak, and may even jump up and down in the frenzy of waiting for a turn to speak. It takes time to learn the give-and-take of free discussion, and the process of learning is often spotted with periods when everybody talks at once. But even adults have such moments and still manage to survive, and to have more discussions. And, after all, children *are* in school to learn such things. Trying and trying and trying again is the essence of learning. If we demand complete order at the beginning of a child's life, we are expecting the children to skip the whole process of learning how to discipline themselves.

If, in the classroom, we concern ourselves less with keeping children quiet and more with the way they view the world, we may achieve the kind of discipline that comes from a sense of being worthwhile and a belief in one's own power to make a good life for oneself. If children feel free to shout out their anger at a real or imagined injustice, they may be less inclined to pick on each other. If they are given ample opportunity to speak, they may be more attentive when other people are talking. If their feelings scream for expression and they are forced to suppress them, to conform to the superimposed pattern of the school, they will be filled with frustration. And they may say, like the youngster in the poverty area of a large city, that "going to school is like being in jail."

Developmental Levels
of Behavior

Though, as students, we have all been exposed to courses on developmental psychology, it is amazing how skillful we are in keeping our knowledge separate from our behavior. We "know" very well that children of eight can sit still comfortably for only short periods of time. Yet I have seen teacher after teacher standing at a chalkboard, asking her children questions, and writing their answers on the board herself. All the while, the children may be begging with every muscle to be permitted to leave their seats and take the short walk to the board. Even if we ignore all the educational values to be found in writing one's own answers, learning to make them legible, taking a stand before a group, and so on, it is still imperative for the eight-year-old to move around at frequent intervals. The same teachers complain about children fidgeting and are very stern with the child who jumps from his seat to wander or to take a poke at another child. These are perceived as "discipline" problems, when they are really biological problems created by a teacher who "knows better."

Self-Control

If we think about it for a moment, we will recognize that discipline is a function of the teaching-learning process. That is, the same factors which are important to the content and methods of teaching are important in achieving control and discipline. This is what we mean when we speak of self-control, and not simply that children should keep quiet because they are told to do so by authority. People who obey the law only because there are penalties for disobedience, or because a policeman is watching, can hardly be considered ideal members of a democracy. As teachers, no matter how far we ourselves fall short of the ideal, we try to guide the development of our students so that they become mentally healthy, self-actualizing personalities. We want to encourage youngsters to be curious, and to pursue their curiosity through the stages of problem definition, data-gathering and solution. We want them to be interested in life problems and to be actively, and skillfully, involved in solving them. This process should keep them busy and interested enough to minimize their need to behave aimlessly, disruptively or destructively.

If a child is not interested in the content of a subject, at the very least there will be no fun in learning; at the most he will, consciously or not, resist learning that subject. He will be called stupid, dull, slow or lazy; he will be beaten, ostracized, ridiculed or deprived; *but he will not learn*. He may, if he has been well-tamed, absorb the content and repeat it for a perfect test paper, but in a very short time it will be as if he has never learned one fact, idea or word that his teacher had forced him to memorize.

If we permit the child to pursue his interests without being rigidly circumscribed by his assigned classroom seat and his textbooks, learning can be a genuine life experience for him rather than a meaningless exercise. Thus, a lesson on the digestive system can become a chance to develop some awareness of what it means to be chronically malnourished. A unit on the American Revolution can become an opportunity to understand contemporary Negro protests. Studying graphs can become an exercise in counting the number of substandard houses in a ghetto and relating it to the high rents paid, as compared to the good housing and lower rents in other parts of the city.

In the process of reading and drawing, interviewing and exploring, comparing and concluding, it is natural to get together in groups to discuss what is happening: Whom did I see? What were the streets like? How did I feel? Why did you say what you did? I was angry; I'm angry now! The free expression of feeling drains off the tension generated by the frustration of living and learning. Practice in verbal expression adds a new dimension to a child's life and increases the avenues of communication available to him. The growing awareness that all behavior is caused builds a firm foundation for a rational approach to defining human problems and contributing to their solution. Interaction becomes a force for control. For, when children are seriously involved in pursuing solutions to real problems, they are inclined to be impatient with interruptions.

Teachers who try to keep complete control over their classes, yet fail to maintain silence and order, may become so zealous about discipline that they forget their real goals. Each class session becomes a battle for ascendancy, with the teacher sometimes winning and sometimes losing. Those children who have been conditioned to remain quiet in the face of frustration, and those who find relevance in what is being taught, will be quiet. But those children who cannot be forced into submissive silence, and those who can see no connection between their lives and their lessons, will present greater and greater problems of discipline.

Realizing that she is failing in her goals, the teacher often becomes defensive and begins to look elsewhere for the causes of her failure. Thus, in certain neighborhoods and with certain ethnic groups, the teachers say that the parents "don't care" about their children's behavior. "Parents do not teach them control," they say. "These children don't respect anyone; they don't respect their parents, so how can they respect their teachers?"

With certain racial groups, teachers blame their failure to teach on the intellectual inferiority of the children. Certain groups are labelled as "naturally" lazy, or "basically" immoral, to account for their school failures and undisciplined behavior. (How easy it is to overlook the fact that the "naturally lazy" groups in our country have traditionally been forced into the hardest, most back-breaking work for the lowest wages.)

It is easy to say that poor children who are not achieving academically, and create problems in the classroom, have no ambition, though the ambitions of poor parents for their children are very often greater than those of middle-class parents.

It is not too difficult to see that problems of discipline arise, not out of controversial subjects, but out of lack of meaning in the school situation. Actually, so-called controversial subjects are the most meaningful matters in our lives: religion, sex, communism, politics, race, divorce, strikes. Take these subjects away, and what is left to stimulate, excite, and interest us or to give us new perspectives and new goals? This is what has happened to school. It has become a world of Dick and Jane and logarithm tables. School becomes simply a preparation for life in the future, ignoring the fact that children are living *now*. Children are not isolated from controversy. They are already involved in it before they ever get to school. What we demand of them when the bell rings is that they suspend their lives, pretend that controversy does not exist, take their seats and open their books. No wonder they are impatient! No wonder they become discipline problems!

Discipline and Intergroup Relations

In our society, people are still often disturbed at the suggestion that they need to consult a psychiatrist. I once asked a physician how his patients reacted when they were referred for psychiatric treatment. He answered that the reaction of the patient seemed to depend on the attitude toward psychiatric treatment of the doctor who referred them. If the doctor felt comfortable about such treatment, and was no more disturbed at the referral than if he were suggesting that the patient see a cardiologist, the patient was likely to accept the suggestion matter-of-factly. The apprehensive, uncomfortable doctor was more likely to elicit a similar response from his patient.

I believe there is an analogy here to the teaching of race relations in the classroom. If the teacher has not come to grips with her own feelings of anxiety about discussing the subject, she is more likely to communicate that feeling to her pupils. If awareness of and sensitivity to race relations are merely part of the interpersonal awareness and sensitivity she wishes to develop in her pupils, she will be better able to guide the children into constructively examining this area of human behavior.

It is undeniable that children may come to class with strong feelings about race learned from their parents, neighbors and friends outside of school. When the subject is introduced, as an aspect of a real problem to be solved, an on-going analysis of a subject studied or an attempt to understand what is happening in the world, the children may very well become involved and emotional in discussing it. But their involvement cannot be mistaken for "disciplinary" behavior. Though their voices may at times become loud, and they may jump to their feet in excitement and anger, they will not engage in the kind of aimlessly destructive or disruptive behavior we generally label disciplinary. On the contrary, it is the anxiety and frustration that arise from keeping racial concerns unverbalized which tend to result in such behavior.

13 The Relation of Intergroup Relations Problems to School Achievement

Self Concept

Most of us have, at some time in our lives, struggled with the problem of self-identity. We have wondered where, in the multiplicity of roles we play and the welter of facades we present to others, to find the peculiar combination of traits and feelings which define us as unique individuals. Generally, the schools we have attended and the teachers we have met have not helped us in this search for self-identity. We were too caught up in school with rote learning and the development of specific skills needed to pass final examinations to spend much time wondering about our essential humanness and what it is that makes us individuals. Now most of the facts we learned in school have been forgotten, and we have settled for a self-image that is more or less acceptable to ourselves and to others. If we have moments of frustration and rebellion, they are usually secret and short-lived, for always tomorrow waits for us and we must don the appropriate mask and go on with the job.

We learned our lesson well: the search for self must not interfere with the program prescribed for us. The discovery of self must be continually postponed so that life—as others have defined it—may go on. And now, as teachers, most of us perpetuate the tradition. In our classrooms, we do not raise the most significant questions. We demand only the "right" answers from our students. And for those who do not play the game, we reserve the label "uneducable."

Most of those whom we dismiss this way are the economically and psychologically deprived in our society. Poor children and minority children, struggling against society's definition of them, are condemned for struggling and penalized by further deprivation. If this seems on the one hand too romantic a perception of discipline problems and low achievement, and on the other hand too harsh a condemnation of the school system, let us look a little more closely at the struggle and its results.

For fifty-one weeks of the year, minority people in our society are taught that they do not matter. They are denied jobs, forced to live in substandard housing and educated in inferior facilities. But one week a year many communities proclaim Negro History Week, and for five days teachers make a point of talking about famous Negro Americans. The response of one child in a slum school of an eastern city illustrates his rejection of this attempt to deny his identity. "What," he demanded, "do I have to do with Ralph Bunche?" It seems to me that what he was really saying was, "I cannot find myself by admiring the accomplishments of Ralph Bunche! I am John Jones. What is there in *me* to admire?"

One teacher, after listing famous Negro Americans for a class of Negro children one day, dismissed her class and escorted them through the halls to the exit. All the way down the hallway, she stopped repeatedly to grab a coat collar, snatch at an arm or shake a small body into line. At one point she admonished the class, "Stop behaving like animals! Act like human beings!" This was in a school that has been characterized as being situated in the Jungle! (The Jungle has become the name of a section of the city which is extremely overcrowded, where the rents are not low and the houses are often unfit for human habitation.) This is a school in which many teachers maintain that, "you can't teach the children much because their parents don't encourage them to learn." (The only time the teachers in the school meet any of the parents is when one is summoned to school for a lecture on a particularly outrageous bit of behavior by her child.)

This is a school where thirty per cent of the teachers are substitutes, only marginally qualified under state teaching requirements. Student teachers visiting the school are horrified at the lack of respect shown by the teachers for the children. Teachers are rude to the students, talk about them in their presence as if they were not there and not infrequently beat them. Every one of these conditions says to the children, "There is nothing about you that is worthwhile." And by rejecting the school in turn, some of the students are replying, "I reject your evaluation of me."

Out of this kind of situation has come the conclusion of many of the young intellectuals in the equality movement that there is no salvation for the Negro in association with whites. They feel that Negroes must find their own identities and that they cannot do so in a so-called integrated situation, because their very proximity to whites is self-destructive. The Negro must, they believe, withdraw from white schools and separately develop the strength that comes from the realization that "I matter," and that "I, fulfilled, am what life is all about!"

I see no salvation in such separation either for Negroes or for whites. The perceptions we have of ourselves must be functional in a social framework. It is unrealistic to try to develop self-awareness in an all-black or an all-white world. In separation lie the seeds of misconception about other groups, and the roots of fear and hostility.

There will always be individuals who find their own confidence by battering at the egos of others. To develop strength shielded from such people means only that our strength must ultimately be tested in their presence. If we separate ourselves from all persons of a particular color, we isolate ourselves not only from the destroyers among them but also from the builders. And we do not, until we rejoin the real world once more, know how to recognize the enemy and render him powerless. Such separation can never, realistically, be complete. Inevitably, majority and minority must share the same technological and economic facilities, respond to the works of the same artists and breathe the same polluted city air. Much of the energy that might be devoted to making the pattern of black-white interrelationships more productive must go into the struggle to maintain separation. There is no doubt in my mind, however, that those same militants are right when they say that black people have the right to determine their own destinies, that they have a right to run their own lives without the management and policymaking of whites. Interracial councils have in the past been slow to make changes and quick to caution patience. Black people must speak in these councils from positions of power and strength or their children, and their children's children, will still be handicapped by lack of equality. Black people are right when they say that most whites, even the self-professed liberals, are not willing to take the only possible stand. But there are some whites who have taken such a stand. To separate the races is to cut off communication between those white people and those black people who want equality now. Such communication is vital if the black people are to develop the power they need and if the committed whites are to continue to teach the majority.

The alternative to separation would seem to be—at least in the educational sphere—to bring people of all groups together, help them become aware of what has happened to them and what continues to happen to them in a world like ours and then to teach them the skills they will need to ameliorate the situation.

An important section in the report made in 1966 by Dr. James S. Coleman of Johns Hopkins University and his associates for the United States Office of Education,[1] deals with children's "sense of control of their environment" and its relation to achievement in school. The conclusion of the researchers was that, "If a child feels that his environment is capricious, or random, or beyond his ability to alter, then he may conclude that attempts to affect it are not worthwhile, and stop trying. . . . The particular relevance of this factor for groups that have been the subject of discrimination is that they have objectively had much less control of their environment than have members of the majority groups." As one would expect, ". . . Negroes and other minority children show much lower sense of control of their environment than do whites."[2] Minority children, then, ". . . in many cases assume that nothing they will do can affect the environment—it will give them benefits or withhold them, but not as a consequence of their own action."[3]

Somehow, we must make minority children believe that their lives can be changed by their own efforts. Somehow, we must teach them the skills that will give them a greater measure of control over their own destinies. And I cannot shake the conviction that we will never be able to do this unless we, as teachers and concerned adults, also become actively involved in effecting social change.

[1] James S. Coleman and others, *Equality of Educational Opportunity* (Washington: Government Printing Office, 1966).
[2] Coleman, pp. 288–89.
[3] Coleman, p. 321.

Effects of Desegregation
on Achievement

There is a growing body of experimental evidence which substantiates the hypothesis that desegregated classes positively affect school achievement, especially for minority youngsters. We cannot say much about experimentally *integrated* classes, because truly integrated classes, especially in public schools, are practically non-existent. But even in the desegregated situation, where we know little or nothing about the quality of interaction between majority and minority groups, there are indications that desegregation is valuable. When we consider, also, that there can be no productive interaction until people of different groups come together physically, we have, I think, ample justification for doing everything in our power to desegregate our schools. Frank Reissman, who has done so much work with deprived youngsters, says, "I know of no place in America where Negroes have obtained quality segregated education. I do know that in the schools where desegregation is occurring, there has been a distinct improvement in the educational performance of Negro children."[4]

Among the surveys and experiments included in the Coleman report are several dealing with the relationship of school achievement to desegregation. One such analysis of short-run results indicated small but positive effects for Negro pupils in classes with whites. The report concludes, "Thus, though the differences are small, and though the degree of integration is not known, there is evident, even in the short run, an effect of school integration on the reading and mathematics achievement of Negro pupils."[5]

The report also states, on the basis of a variety of analyses, that, "Attributes of other students account for far more variation in the achievement of minority group children than do any attributes of school facilities and slightly more than do attributes of staff."[6] There is nothing startlingly new about this conclusion, since we have previous sociological evidence of the effect of social class segregation on aspirations and achieve-

[4] Frank Reissman, "Ebb and Flow in the School Integration Movement," *Integrated Education*, 4:8–18 (October–November, 1966).

[5] Coleman, p. 29.

[6] Coleman, p. 302.

ment.[7] "In general," the Coleman report continues, "as the educational aspirations and backgrounds of fellow students increase, the achievement of minority children increases."[8]

A closer analysis of the data suggests that desegregation has the most profound effect on children from disadvantaged backgrounds.[9] This is borne out in a study made by Dr. David J. Armor, Assistant Professor of Sociology at Harvard University, for the 1967 report of the United States Commission on Civil Rights. It says, "For the Negro male, it is the qualified, bright student from a lower class background and in a more deprived school, who is aided most by integration (or, conversely, hurt most by segregation)."[10]

In analyzing the qualities of the student body to determine which factors were affecting achievement, it became clear, according to the Coleman report, that, "The educational backgrounds and aspirations of fellow students appear to provide a facilitating or amplifying effect on the achievement of a student independent of his own background."[11]

In examining the effects of racial composition specifically on achievement, Coleman notes that as the proportion of whites to non-whites increases, *the achievement of students in each racial group increases.* He concludes, ultimately, that this "comes not from racial composition per se, but from the better educational background and higher educational aspirations that are, on the average, found among white students."[12] When we examine this conclusion in the light of the Coleman report's findings on educational facilities and programs, we see that, indeed, the advantages to minorities of associating with the majority do not lie in any inherent racial superiority.

> Just as minority groups tend to have less access to physical facilities that seem to be related to academic achievement, so too they have less access to curricular and extracurricular programs that would seem to have such a relationship.

[7] Alan B. Wilson, "Residential Segregation of Social Classes and Aspirations of High School Boys," *American Sociological Review*, 24:836–845 (1959).

[8] Coleman, pp. 302–3.

[9] Coleman, p. 304.

[10] *Racial Isolation in the Public Schools; a report of the U.S. Commission on Civil Rights* (Washington, 1967), Appendices, 2:146.

[11] Coleman, p. 305.

[12] Coleman, p. 307.

Secondary school Negro students are less likely to attend schools that are regionally accredited. . . . Negro and Puerto Rican pupils have less access to college preparatory curriculums and to accelerated curriculums; Puerto Ricans have less access to vocational curriculums as well. . . . Finally, white students in general have more access to a more fully developed program of extracurricular activities, in particular those which might be related to academic matters (debate teams, for example, and student newspapers).[13]

For those who point to differential achievement test scores between minority and majority pupils as evidence of racial inferiority, the real cause of the differential is identified: "If a large part of the effect of a school on a student is accounted for by the achievement level of other students in the school, then in a segregated system, if one group begins at an educationally impoverished level, it will tend to remain at that level."[14]

Evidence supporting this conclusion lies in the situations we see around us. Sol Gordon, Director of Project Beacon in New York City, sums up ghetto education tersely, "In no large city in the country has a school board succeeded in educating the masses of Negro, Puerto Rican, and Mexican-American children who reside in the slums. 'Less than 20% reading at grade level' is the prevalent portrait of our inner city Harlems."[15]

Again and again, researchers into the effects of educational programs on minority youngsters find evidence that the causes of low achievement lie not in the home, not in some inherent disability, but in the quality of the segregated education situation. Workers in the Harlem Youth Project (HARYOU), headed by Dr. Kenneth B. Clark, Professor of Psychology at the College of the City of New York, report,

Specifically, there is no conclusive evidence to demonstrate a consistent relationship between "poor homes" or "broken homes" and the ability of a child to learn to read. . . . Furthermore, the fact that 85 percent of the children in the public schools in Harlem are retarded in reading and arith-

13 Coleman, p. 12.

14 Coleman, p. 310.

15 Sol Gordon, "The Bankruptcy of Ghetto Education," *Intergroup Education*, 4:32–34 (October–November, 1966).

metic cannot be logically explained as being due to social and personal pathology. Not all . . . are from poor or broken homes.[16]

A study in New Rochelle, New York—a suburban community with a heterogeneous population—reported success in desegregating schools, measured by the reading comprehension scores of the children. It was found that Negro children transferred to white schools achieved at least as well as the other children in the schools. When one considers the many problems these transfer students must have had to deal with, to achieve as well as the other students is undoubtedly an indication of success. "The challenges to be met by these youngsters were several: adjustment to new school staff and physical surroundings, the novelty of being bused to and from school, anxiety and apprehension as to acceptance by a largely white peer group . . ." Only reading scores were used as a measure of achievement. A multitude of other possible effects of desegregation were not directly measured, such as "changes in self-esteem, motivation, and effort."[17]

A citizens' committee appointed by the California State Board of Education concluded that, "children of equal basic ability are not learning language skills as well in those schools that have a large Negro enrollment as in the schools with a predominantly Caucasian enrollment."[18] The committee suspected that, because buildings, teacher qualifications and teacher turnover rates did not differ in Negro and white areas, the factors causing differences in achievement "reflected in part different attitudes held by both teachers and students in different parts of the city." The implication was that teachers had different standards of achievement and set different tasks for Negro and white students. To sum up, "The committee found that de facto segregation has a profound effect on the education of our children. This is evident in the performance of their academic achievement, in their relationships with their fellow students, in their views of themselves, and in their future careers and responsibilities as citizens."

[16] "Educational Excellence in Harlem," *Integrated Education*, 2:13–20 (June–July, 1964).

[17] T. G. Wolman, "Learning Effects of Integration in New Rochelle," Integrated Education, 2:30–31 (December, 1964–January, 1965).

[18] Citizens' Committee, "School Segregation in Berkeley," Integrated Education, 2:43–46 (April–May, 1964).

Dr. Gerald S. Lesser, Director of the Laboratory of Human Development at Harvard University, conducted a study over a five-year period with young children from Negro, Puerto Rican, Chinese and Jewish families in New York City. He and his colleagues report:

> Each group included children both from racially-imbalanced and relatively balanced schools. . . . For every one of the four abilities measured—verbal ability, reasoning, numerical ability, and space conceptualization—the children from the more integrated schools and neighborhoods showed significantly superior performance when compared to the children from racially imbalanced schools and neighborhoods.[19]

In Louisville, Kentucky, desegregation resulted in better performance not only for Negro youngsters, but also for their white classmates. The report found that ". . . substantial gains were shown in scholastic achievement, with both Negro and white children making these gains."[20]

As far back as 1955, Dr. Otto Klineberg, the anthropologist, found that intelligence test scores increase as children move from an inferior educational situation to a better one.[21] But we are now faced with the contemporary picture of children in inferior educational situations achieving at low levels, and whose low achievement is being widely used as a reason for further limiting their educational opportunity.

[19] Gerald S. Lesser, "Some Effects of Segregation and Desegregation," *Integrated Education*, 2:20–26 (June–July, 1964).
[20] Quoted by Lesser, op. cit.
[21] Otto Klineberg, *Negro Intelligence and Selective Migration* (New York: Columbia University Press, 1955).

Note: No attempt has been made in this chapter to present a complete review of the research in the field. Rather, studies which represent the general tenor of the most recent research have been reported.

IV "We must cover the course of study"

Most of the textbooks and other curricular materials we use do not deal with the intergroup problems facing us today. To suggest that all this material be discarded is neither practical nor necessary. Much of it includes facts and concepts that we undoubtedly do want to continue to teach our students. A more realistic, and possibly more effective, alternative for the teacher is to learn to fill in the gaps and omissions in standard material herself.

The aim of this section is to use familiar materials from several subject matter areas and grade levels to show how the teacher can use similar materials to teach intergroup relations. Chapters 14 through 19 are each based on a particular book that is used widely in the schools. In each case the book's text is used as a framework for exploring intergroup concepts. Wherever the material lends itself to inclusion of an intergroup fact, comparison with a contemporary event or development of a social-psychological insight, interpolations are suggested. Where the basic reference book tends to reinforce stereotypes and perpetuate misconceptions about groups, corrections are proposed.

The net result of this approach will, I hope, be a presentation of curriculum materials which teachers generally feel are of proven value, materials with which they feel comfortable, materials which represent the "sense" of our culture and our cumulative knowledge. But these materials have been expanded to allow for the teaching of intergroup sensitivities. Teachers, familiar with the basic material, are given clues for further development of their subject matter areas to make what they teach more immediately pertinent to the pressing social problems of today.

The basic assumption of this approach is that there is no system of knowledge that does not have significance for human interaction, and that scholarship which is divorced from concern with man will be sterile and, ultimately, dangerous. For, though some researchers like to say that the pursuit of "pure" knowledge knows no morality, they cannot obscure the fact that the pursuers are men, and that the choices they make are rooted in their own conceptions of morality. It is men who decide which questions need to be answered. It is men who decide upon the methods of research. The very curiosity of the scientist, which is supposedly uncontaminated by moral strictures and free to carry him into uncharted areas of knowledge, is conditioned by a lifetime of experiences to go in some directions and not in others.

When the minds of men study, the study is related to those men. Every area of knowledge at some point affects, and is affected by, man and his interrelationships. The scientist who is not deluded by the myth of complete objectivity—the artist is never so deluded!—is much better equipped to see and to avoid the pitfalls into which men's choices may lead.

14 Shakespeare's *Julius Caesar*— Teaching Intergroup Relations with a Traditional Text

"The study of English in the secondary schools is particularly adapted to helping young people achieve the qualities of good personal living and social competence."[1] This is the observation of one of the largest school systems in our country, an observation grown out of the work of practicing teachers and school administrators. Yet who can deny that "good personal living" and "social competence" can be developed only within the larger social context of contemporary life? Concern with existing social problems, as well as with problems of individual adjustment, must inevitably be an integral part of the course of study in English.

William Shakespeare's play, *Julius Caesar*,[2] is one of the few classics prescribed for study in most secondary schools. "About 60 per cent of the courses of study specify that *Julius Caesar* be taught in grade 9, 10, or 11."[3] It is probable that the play is read in other schools which do not make it mandatory. And *Julius Caesar* is a superb source of knowledge and insights which the young people who study it may not have the opportunity to acquire elsewhere.

We are forever pointing out to youngsters that Shakespeare was an astute observer of human behavior. Such an observation can have relatively little significance for the high school student if he interprets it—as he so often does—to mean that Shake-

[1] Department of Public Instruction, *Bulletin No. 280*, Harrisburg, Pennsylvania, 1952.

[2] Helge Kokeritz and Charles T. Prouty, eds., *The Yale Shakespeare,* revised (New Haven, 1959).

[3] Arno Jewett, *English Language Arts in American High Schools* (Washington, D.C.: Office of Education) Bulletin 1958, 13:66.

speare created characters who resemble real people. The student must be led to the next step in understanding by observing in the development of Shakespearean characters traits of human behavior which he may recognize in himself and in other people.

Crowd Behavior

Of particular significance for human relations is the ability to recognize in the characters—and in human beings generally—both rational and irrational motives for behavior. If young people are taught to accept and understand the existence of irrationality in themselves and others, they are more likely to be able to control it. The large component of irrationality in ethnic prejudice makes understanding of this universal human propensity basic in any attempt to improve intergroup relations.

A stunning example of irrationality is found in Shakespeare's dramatization of crowd behavior. At the beginning of Act III, Scene 2, the Roman populace demands an explanation for the death of Caesar. "We will be satisfied," they cry, "let us be satisfied." They seem at first quite reasonable, prepared to listen to Brutus and then to Cassius and to "compare their reasons." Listening to Brutus, the crowd agrees that the murder of Caesar was justified by his ambitions to enslave them. Moved by a popular and eloquent politician, the crowd gives no thought to the possible use of law as an alternative to execution without trial. They accept the patriotic motives Brutus professes as his only reason for killing another politician. So convinced are they of his patriotism and altruism that they offer him the position of Caesar. When Antony rises to speak, they murmur, " 'Twas best he speak no harm of Brutus here!" Before hearing another side of the story, the crowd is already convinced that "This Caesar was a tyrant," and that Rome is well rid of him.

Before Antony's speech is over, the crowd has been swayed to the opposite extreme and is convinced that "Caesar has had great wrong," and that "there will a worse come in his place." Soon they are calling Caesar's assassins traitors, and are ready to "Burn! Fire! Kill! Slay! Let not a traitor live,"—especially after hearing that they are the beneficiaries of Caesar's will.

In modern times, crowds have behaved very similarly, moved this way and that by gifted speakers who know how to play upon emotions. Greed, anger and fear, normally held in check, are often unleashed in the anonymity of a crowd. Recently a new little community in a northeastern city saw a crowd of some five hundred normally law-abiding citizens throw stones at the home of a family with two small children and at the police officers who were trying to protect them. The family was middle-class and Negro; they were excitedly planning the furnishings and landscaping of their new home when the first rock was thrown. It was a long time before they were able to enjoy the house that was to be the fulfillment of a long-cherished dream.

But what of the crowd that threw the rocks? Some time after the incident, at a meeting called by community leaders appalled by the incident, a man who had been in the crowd got up to speak. "I don't know why I did such a thing," he said. "I can't tell you how sorry I am about it. I just seemed to get caught up in everything that was going on around me. And I guess I didn't want any Negroes in my town. But I shouldn't have become a part of a mob. How could all that have been prevented?"

That man did not understand himself. He had surprised himself by his own behavior. He had never considered the consequences of such behavior. He had never given serious thought to how he felt about Negroes, why he felt the way he did, how prevalent such feelings are or how Negro people feel in a society where others reject them just because they are Negroes. Thus, faced with a crisis situation, the feelings in the crowd had touched a responsive chord in him, and he had followed blindly. The parallel with *Julius Caesar* could not be clearer.

The Effect of Fear and Guilt
on Judgment

There are other aspects of character development in Shakespeare's play which may help the student to isolate and solve problems in intergroup relations. It would be easy to miss the significance of the few lines dramatizing how fear and guilt can interfere with knowledge and sound judgment. In Act II,

Scene 1, the conspirators are so nervous that they cannot even agree on the direction from which the sun rises. In Act II, Scene 2, Portia is so disturbed that she scolds a boy for not doing her bidding before she has told him what she wants him to do.

These minute incidents demonstrate a basic concept in intergroup relations. Many Negroes, afraid of the power of white people and mindful of the treatment Negroes have received at the hands of whites, perceive every white person as a potential source of pain—ranging from a social snub to outright violence. That there are many white people who have devoted their lives to improving the lot of colored people, and that many whites perceive Negroes as human beings just like themselves are facts often overlooked because of fear.

We can often see evidence in white people of how guilt influences judgment of other racial groups. For example, we are exhorted every day not to practice discrimination and to exemplify the concept of democracy in our behavior. These appeals conflict with what many people have learned all their lives—that other groups are inferior to them. Believing in democracy on the one hand and unable to overcome their emotional attachment to their early learnings on the other, they often react by feeling guilty about rejecting other groups. And because it is very difficult to acknowledge guilt, individuals often become angry in order to relieve their guilt feelings; the object of this anger is often the very groups the white person has been exhorted to accept. How is one to justify this behavior rationally? In order to give the appearance of rationality, so greatly valued in our culture, many people are compelled to accept as facts only negative traits in other groups and to reject or ignore the positive traits. Thus guilt interferes with our acquisition of knowledge and distorts our judgment.

Lack of Knowledge and Prejudgment

Lack of knowledge about people, in combination with myth and superstition, leads to prejudgments which interfere with recognition and acceptance of individuals on their own merits. Caesar's remark about Cassius ("Yond Cassius has a lean and hungry look . . . such men are dangerous"), though Shakespeare makes it an accurate one for dramatic purposes, is the type of prejudgment which is often made across racial, religious and nationality-group lines. Just as Caesar based his judgment on Cassius' physical appearance, white people often respond to individuals in a certain way only because their skin is dark.

This visible cue of skin color, the myths in our society concerning people with dark skin, the ignorance of white people about Negro people because they have so few opportunities to get to know them as equals—all these factors contribute to a negative prejudgment of Negro individuals when white people *do* come into contact with them. Caesar's judgment of Cassius is reminiscent of people's persistent belief in the pseudo-science of physiognomy, just as the white person's rejection of Negroes is often based on discredited 19th-century "scientific" writings whose influence persists to the present day.

Dichotomous Thinking

Brutus, confronted with the conspirators' arguments that Caesar is dangerous and so must be murdered, defines his problem in terms of alternatives: his honor as a Roman as opposed to the murder of his friend. He perceives no other possible courses of action. In human terms, both choices are undesirable; the significant thing is that Brutus feels compelled to choose between the two. This is the way many people behave in the area of intergroup relations: they see the alternatives as intermarriage on the one hand and the subjugation of the minority group on the other. They have no awareness of the many levels and areas of possible interaction between these two extremes.

In intergroup relations, we are at present concerned with developing optimal interaction between different racial, religious, and nationality groups. This means the development of awareness in people of different groups that they have problems in common which can be solved only by breaking down the barriers to communication across group lines. These barriers to communication—ignorance of the other group, fear, lack of skill in working together with people of other races, religions or national origin—discourage most of us from re-evaluating our attitudes toward other groups. And so members of majority groups continue to act as if there were only two possible choices in their social attitudes, and to choose the one which for them represents safety and a perpetuation of the *status quo*.

This kind of either-or thinking can be seen in the attitudes of minority people too. It is particularly evident now among many Americans who come to the mainland from Puerto Rico. Soon after their arrival, they become aware of the discrimination practiced against dark-skinned Americans. Because many Puerto Ricans are also dark-skinned, they feel the need to distinguish themselves from dark-skinned mainlanders, in the hope that they will not become victims of the same treatment.

Recognizing that their language is their most obvious distinguishing characteristic, Puerto Ricans often decide that the choice is to speak only Spanish or to learn English and be treated like mainland Negroes. This kind of thinking ignores such factors as the need for English in order to work with other members of the community to improve living and working conditions and in order to advance in education and economic status. Fluency in English does not preclude perpetuating Spanish language and customs and contributing to the diversity of American culture. But as long as Puerto Ricans regard English and Spanish as mutually exclusive alternatives, they are immobilized, and their economic, social and psychological development will be seriously impeded. The ultimate result of Brutus' choice was his own death.

Believing the People We Love

Most of us acquire our first attitudes from people we love and who love us. Before we are able to judge these opinions maturely, we accept them without question. It is in this way that we learn the behaviors and attitudes which society expects of us. However, as we mature and develop the ability to evaluate our early learnings, we may change the attitudes and behavior our parents taught us. This is a difficult thing to do, for we may feel that we are rejecting our parents when we reject their beliefs. The job of the teacher is to help young people realize that, as they learn and experience more, and as the world changes, they must continually reevaluate their attitudes and behavior in the light of their increasing knowledge, skill and sensitivity. And they can do this even while they continue to love and appreciate the parents who reared them.

Far too many of us continue even as adults to follow blindly the people we love or admire. Ligarius exemplifies this (Act II, Scene 1):

> ... I follow you,
> To do I know not what; but it sufficeth
> That Brutus leads me on.

A scientific, rational skepticism is the essence of clear thinking and sound decision-making. Even those we love are fallible, and our love need not be diminished when we discover this fallibility.

Attitudes Toward Authority

In Act I, Scene 1, tribunes stop workingmen on the street and roughly ask what right they have to be walking in the street in holiday clothes on a working day. The workingmen, though careful not to resist obviously, slyly poke fun at these authorities. It would be interesting to compare this scene with the behavior of modern police officers and the attitudes of citizens toward the police in our country. The old stereotype of the tough, stupid, dishonest "cop" is no longer acceptable in a democratic society. Yet aspects of the stereotype persist and cause difficulties between the police and the public.

One of the difficulties involves the relationship between minority-group people and the police. For example, large concentrations of Negro people in the poorer areas of some of our metropolitan centers have given rise to the misconception that most crimes are committed by Negroes—and, further, that Negroes have inborn criminal tendencies. Many white police officers believe this, too, and their belief influences their treatment of Negro citizens. Expecting Negroes to be up to no good, policemen are much more likely to stop a Negro on the street, and to question him discourteously, than they are to detain a white. They will more often arrest Negro people "on suspicion," a suspicion which is at least partly a function of prejudgment of all Negro people. They will often show little interest in crimes committed against Negroes by Negroes, because of their devaluation of Negroes as human beings.

Negro police officers may be harsher with Negro offenders or suspects than they are with whites, for fear of being accused of leniency toward "their own" people. Many Negro police officers are harsher with Negro citizens because they feel that every violation by a Negro is a reflection on all Negroes—and on themselves.

As a result of these attitudes and behavior patterns, Negro people very often react with great hostility toward policemen. This hostility is likely to be directed against *all* police officers, not only because some of them treat Negro people unfairly, but also because they are symbols of a society which has traditionally relegated Negro people to a position of inferiority. Police administrators are beginning to be aware of these problems and many are developing extensive programs designed to improve police-community relations. Others, however, are refusing to admit that they have any responsibility to help improve police-minority group relations.

The subtle hostility directed against the tribunes by the Roman populace might very profitably be examined in the light of contemporary democratic government and the attitudes of free people toward symbols of authority.

Inner Conflict and Hostility

> ... poor Brutus, with himself at war,
> Forgets the shows of love to other men.

So Brutus (Act I, Scene 2) explains to Cassius that he was not really angry as his behavior might have indicated, but that he was struggling with an inner conflict which made his overt behavior unfriendly. Even his beloved Portia is not safe from his hostility. She rebukes him (Act I, Scene 2):

> And when I asked you what the matter was,
> You star'd upon me with ungentle looks.
> I urg'd you further; then you scratched your head,
> And too impatiently stamp'd with your foot;
> Yet I insisted, yet you answer'd not,
> But with an angry wafter of your hand
> Gave sign for me to leave you.

There is further evidence that Brutus was torn with conflict. In Act II, Scene 1, already prepared to join the conspiracy, he calls it monstrous, and speaks of the shame of it. Later in the scene, he talks of the "even virtue of our enterprise."

Hostility against others can often be explained in terms of an individual's inner conflicts and frustrations. The man who worries about his inability to get ahead cannot vent his feelings of frustrated anger on employers, relatives or friends. They will not stand for it. But a group of people in his environment who are generally rejected by his associates constitutes a "safe" target for his anger. But he must seem reasonable about his hostility, so he explains his lack of financial success as the fault of "all those pushy foreigners" who are getting the good jobs.

We have, of course, extended our analysis several steps beyond the original example of Brutus' unfriendliness, but the basic principle of unresolved conflict and frustration manifesting themselves in object-directed hostility and aggression is the same. People with some insight into the motivation for such irrational hostility may at least be persuaded to control their overt hostile behavior.

Devaluing other people is a mechanism used by many who can overcome their feelings of inferiority only by continually pointing out the inferiority of others. Cassius, who could not bear to see someone else in a superior position, takes great trouble to detail the weaknesses and ills of Caesar, even going so far as to label him a coward because he shook when he had a fever (Act I, Scene 2); thus Cassius "proved" himself more worthy of exalted position than Caesar. The individual who can point to whole groups of people in our society—Negroes, Puerto Ricans, Jews, Catholics, "foreigners" and "prove" their inferiority, can by inference maintain his own superiority. The person who is confident of his own worth, and who feels safe and accepted for what he is, need not depend on the denigration of others for a sense of his own value.

Fear and Hostility

All kinds of strange happenings are interpreted by Casca as signs of the evil times and warnings of the danger which Caesar represents to Rome (Act I, Scene 3). Cicero makes an observation worthy of a contemporary psychologist. "But men may construe things after their fashion," he says, "clean from the purpose of the things themselves." In just this way, we often use facts and statistics to justify prejudice and discrimination, and sometimes interpret actions we oppose as signs of the fulfillment of our worst fears.

We may insist that the high Negro crime rate in large cities means that Negroes have "natural" criminal tendencies. The deteriorated appearance of many Negro neighborhoods becomes, to many, irrefutable testimony that Negroes do not care about keeping their homes in good repair. And so it goes: desegregation will cause interracial violence; employing minority-group people on the basis of merit will cause workers to leave their jobs; having a Negro family as a next-door neighbor will cause deterioration of neighborhood standards of cleanliness and morality. We prophesy doom if we must make changes in our way of life. Our fears, not our reason, lead us to these conclusions, just as superstitious fear is used by characters in the play to justify the conspiracy against Caesar.

Unconscious Motivation in Human Behavior

Unconscious motivation underlies much of our behavior. The reasons we propose for rejecting whole groups of people may sound reasonable and even acceptable in our culture, but the real motivations often lie in our own conflicts, frustrations and needs. The theory has been advanced that the rejection of Jews in this country may be partly a result of our unconscious fear and hatred of the impersonal, unfriendly city whose crowds suffocate us, whose advertising makes us want things we cannot have and whose competition threatens us with destruction. The Jew, whose historical experiences have made him a city dweller, may have become for many the symbol of the hated city.

Shakespeare gives us a glimpse of his awareness of unconscious motivation in the behavior of Brutus. Arguing with himself (Act II, Scene 1), Brutus admits that Caesar has done nothing wrong and that he has "no personal cause to spurn at him." But, his argument continues, if Caesar is crowned, he may abuse his immense power; therefore, he had better be killed *before* he does something terrible. We cannot help wondering here what really motivates Brutus to join the conspirators. Can it be envy? His own desire for power? His appreciation of Cassius' flattery? It must be something more than just the desire to save Rome from a tyrant—for Caesar is not a tyrant, and has not even accepted the crown.

Often we respond to direct stimuli without realizing that we are doing so or what our response indicates. So Decius says (Act II, Scene 1) of Caesar:

> But when I tell him he hates flatterers,
> He says, he does, being then most flattered.

Just as Caesar prides himself on his immunity to flattery, many of us are quick to maintain our complete freedom from prejudice even while we are betraying our negative attitudes toward other groups. The person who prophesies serious trouble if a Negro teacher is assigned to an all-white school, the student who would not think of sharing a table in the school cafeteria with members of another racial group, the person who thinks that all Catholics agree on every issue—these people have been influenced by the pattern of prejudice and discrimination which runs through the fabric of our society. In one way or another, we have all been influenced by it—it is evidence of a lack of self-insight to insist that such a pervasive force in our culture has had no effect on our thinking and feeling.

Rationalization

Rationalization is the substitution of socially acceptable reasons for the real reasons which motivate our behavior. Because reason and logic are so highly valued in our culture, we are expected to have clear and acceptable reasons for what we do. However, we often do not know the real reasons for our behavior, and often, too, our motives are in conflict with what society considers good or right.

Shakespeare's Caesar exemplifies well how rationalization operates in human beings, and offers a clue to the way it is used to justify prejudice and discrimination. Though himself unsuperstitious, Caesar is persuaded by Calpurnia's forebodings not to go to the Senate. He agrees, he says, ". . . for thy humor . . . not for my fear." Later he confides to Decius that:

> . . . on her knee
> [She] Hath begg'd that I will stay at home today.

It is important to note how quickly Caesar accedes to Calpurnia's whim. Only the temptation of the crown and

Decius' intimation that Rome will laugh at a man governed by his wife's fears lure Caesar to the Senate. But we cannot help sensing Caesar's underlying fear and reluctance, and we understand his first impulse to use Calpurnia's pleas as an excuse to avoid danger.

In just this way, we look for plausible reasons to reject members of other groups in order to give our fears an appearance of logic and acceptability. "Cleanliness," we say, "is important." Therefore, those who are not clean are inferior. We do not ask why some people are not clean. We do not wonder how our need for cleanliness developed and why the same need has not developed in the same way in some other people. We even go so far as to assume that, if *many* people in a particular ethnic group have not developed this need, all members of the group are dirty and are to be rejected. The rejection of whole groups of people is a result not of such secondary considerations, but of fear, hatred and hostility toward them. Rejection on the grounds of cleanliness is largely rationalization.

Self-Hatred
Some minority group people are so affected by the hatred, denigration and discrimination they experience that they come to believe in the prevailing image of themselves. Social psychologists have observed this phenomenon in many minority-group individuals and have called it "group self-hate." Portia reveals a similar conviction when she says,

> How hard it is for women to keep counsel. (Act II, Scene 2)

Why does she think that women are less able than men to control their emotions? Evidently her society has taught her, as ours has taught us, that women are less stable emotionally than men. Science had disproven this idea, but it persists in men and women alike.

Anger and Hostility
The Roman mob, aroused by Antony's subtle skill, seems to have utterly abandoned rationality and to be venting its anger on anyone in its path. The crowd stops Cinna the poet (Act III, Scene 3), and asks him whether he is married or a bachelor. When he implies that he is happy to be a bachelor, he is threatened with violence—presumably by a married man. We

can only imagine the reaction of a bachelor in the crowd had Cinna answered that he was happy to be married. It is obvious that the mob is merely searching for a reason to attack him. (Rationalization again!) When he protests that he is not Cinna the conspirator, the mob responds:

> It is no matter, his name's Cinna; pluck but his name
> out of his heart, and turn him going.

When he insists that he is Cinna the poet, the mob's response is:

> Tear him for his bad verses . . .

Emotionally aroused and perhaps feeling guilty, the mob finds the innocent Cinna to blame for a treachery they had applauded a short while earlier.

There is an excellent parallel in our modern intergroup relations. Gunnar Myrdal, the Swedish sociologist, points out in *An American Dilemma* that Americans suffer from a national feeling of guilt. Reared to believe in the precepts of democracy and equality, they treat large groups of people as inferiors and subject them to indignities and deprivations because of their ethnic-group membership. The resultant feeling of guilt, and the anxiety it arouses, find relief in anger directed against the innocent victims of prejudice and discrimination. The mobs of white people who throw stones at the home of a Negro family very often find that abusing a minority-group family relieves them temporarily of the guilt and anger which their conflicts and frustrations have engendered.

Ceremonials and Testimonials

"There are no tricks in plain and simple faith," says Brutus (Act IV, Scene 1) of the ceremonial politeness Cassius practices to disguise a lack of warmth and openness. We are reminded of the majority-group person, eager to convince the minority person of his friendship, who delivers irrelevant and awkward testimonials to the "industry" or "wonderful home life" or "natural musical ability" of "your people." Sometimes the testimonial is less specific. A white person may assure a Negro that "I think your people are wonderful"; a non-Jew may confide to a Jew that "Some of my best friends are Jews." These testimonials to the minority, like the "enforced ceremony" Brutus talks about, are met with little enthusiasm by those who would prefer acceptance as individuals to hollow reassurance that their race or religion is "admired."

Effecting Social Change

The plot of *Julius Caesar*—dealing as it does with murder and war as methods for effecting change in government—is a convenient framework for discussing alternative methods to bring about social change with the least amount of destruction. In intergroup relations, we often speak of constructive conflict, and of means to channel this conflict toward desirable goals. For example, the custom in our southern states of refusing Negroes service at chain-store lunch counters was long recognized as deplorable. College students organized to discuss the problem and ways to solve it. They decided that firm and peaceful insistence on service would draw the attention of the general public to the problem in a dramatic way, and that nonviolent response to taunts, threats, attacks and imprisonment would avoid injury and serve to keep public attention focused on the issue itself. This policy of self-discipline and refusal to indulge in hostility resulted in a change in the policy of several chain stores and, more broadly, a modification in the cultural patterns of many southern cities. Some conflict was inevitable, but the fact remains that major social change was effected without extreme violence.

Methods of Teaching Intergroup Relations with Julius Caesar

Rewriting the Play Students who are facile with language and who develop a good understanding of the play may like to try their hands at rewriting the play—or particular scenes—by attributing different motives to a character, and showing how his altered behavior changes the outcome.

Suppose, for example, that Brutus had had somewhat more insight into himself. Suppose he had been less susceptible to flattery, less easily moved to believe Caesar dangerous or somewhat more aware of his own political ambitions. How might he have dealt wth Cassius? How might he have used his influence to prevent tyranny without resorting to murder and civil war? How might he have developed this awareness of his own motives? (How may people today learn more about themselves and why they act as they do?)

Suppose many people in the crowd listening to Antony's speech had refused to be swayed by his emotional appeal. Suppose that leaders had emerged from the crowd who wanted to deal with the murder of Caesar by legal measures. How might the play have ended?

Some children might enjoy rewriting parts of the play in contemporary—even colloquial—language. This often results in greater identification with the characters, and encourages personal comparisons like, "If I were Brutus . . ." and "If I were Antony, I would have considered the potential terrible consequences of my funeral oration before I gave it. But then, I would have had to be more interested in the safety of Rome and its citizens, than in being revenged for the death of a friend." It also encourages comparison of the characters with famous modern figures and may lead to observations on such things as Gandhi's method of inducing social change and the influence of Gandhi on America's Martin Luther King.

(One group of students who rewrote and performed the balcony scene from *Romeo and Juliet* in colloquial language, and performed it for other students and faculty, discovered the humor in the scene which few present-day interpreters recognize, but which must have delighted Shakespeare's audiences.)

Questions for Discussion Class discussion of such questions as "Which character are you most like, or most unlike?" can encourage both greater understanding of many facets of the play and deeper self-knowledge. A student who recognizes his own tendency to believe in supernatural signs and portents might be encouraged to explore the widely-held belief that "God made different races because He wanted them separate." Such subjects also make excellent themes for compositions.

Another question for discussion might be, "Which character do you dislike most?" The students might think Cassius, the man who blamed his own lack of eminence on the success of Caesar, or Brutus, who betrayed a friend without recognizing his own motivations for doing so, so repugnant that they could profitably be led to explore the high incidence of such behavior traits in human beings. They might even begin to see in themselves tendencies to displace their own frustrations onto other people; and they might begin to accept the theory that many of their own motivations are unconscious.

Or the students may have noticed the similarity of Roman senatorial togas to the dress of some African representatives to the United Nations. They might consider why Afro-Americans do not wear the toga, and thus come to some conclusions about the influence of culture—historical and contemporary—on human behavior. They might come to doubt that there are "Negro" characteristics, that *all* Puerto Ricans are "born" irresponsible or that *all* Jews have an "instinct" for business.

Role-Playing Rather than rewriting the play the students might prefer to act out scenes like those in the play, spontaneously and without a text, in order to gain greater understanding of the motives and emotions of the characters. A crowd responding to a patriotic speech like Antony's is especially well-suited to this approach. One student might take the role of the orator, while ten or fifteen others make up the crowd. Several members of the crowd would have the roles of making verbal responses to the speech and thus inciting the crowd into becoming a mob. The words spoken by all the players should be spontaneous, guided only by the character descriptions and the scene set by the rest of the class. Those not participating would watch for consistency of character development, the relation of cause and effect in the characters' behavior and indications of the underlying motives of behavior. After a scene has been played, role players and observers can discuss the scene. Observers and participants might change places, replay the scene differently and discuss both versions.

Small-Group Activities While the class is studying *Julius Caesar,* several students might be assigned to search newspapers and magazines for contemporary events analogous to the situations in the play. The group may either present its findings for class discussion or report on the events while the rest of the class listens and comments.

Another group might be assigned short stories, novels, plays and poems with similar plots or characters to those of the play. They could summarize these materials for the class or read excerpts aloud as a basis for discussion.

A group interested in historical research might trace the history of the toga-like garment worn by contemporary Africans, comparing it to the dress of eastern Indians, and investigating the possibility of a link between this garment and the Roman toga.

Diaries A student with creative talent might write a diary for one of the play's characters, revealing in it the doubts, conflicts, fears and unspoken motivations which may be inferred from the play. Another student might write a summary of the play and an account of the characters from the point of view of a Roman of the time who was not an active participant in the events. Still another might write about the events as if he were from Gaul or Germany and had heard about the events in Rome from passing travelers.[4]

[4] Adapted from "Teaching Intergroup Relations with a Traditional Text," *The Journal of Intergroup Relations*, 3:220–236 (Summer, 1962).

15 United States History— The Colonial Period

An Explanatory Note

The discussion of colonial America which follows is organized very loosely around the section devoted to this period in the reference text.[1] My intent in this and the chapters which follow is to use the account in the reference text as a point of departure for the introduction of intergroup concepts. If an historical fact or idea in the text appears to have relevance for intergroup relations, it is discussed, expanded, and related specifically to current intergroup problems. Quotations taken verbatim from the text are identified by quotation marks in this and subsequent chapters.

Because American history is an integral part of elementary, secondary and college curricula, an understanding of the relation between our early history and our present intergroup difficulties would seem to be valuable for most teachers. Given this basic knowledge, teachers can use their traditional skill and ingenuity to develop new ways to involve students in learning intergroup relations.

Interreligious Relations

The Mayflower Compact, an excerpt from which opens the chapter on colonial history in the reference text, is dramatic evidence of how far we have progressed in 350 years toward intergroup tolerance. The Plymouth colony was founded, in the words of the Compact, "for the glory of God and the advancement of the Christian faith." The Mayflower Pilgrims, intent upon their own religious troubles and fearing for their own rights, began with the wording of the Mayflower Compact to exclude from their consideration the rights of other religious

[1] Richard C. Wade, Howard B. Wilder and Louise C. Wade, *A History of the United States* (Boston: Houghton Mifflin Company, 1966).

groups. And thus "the general good of the colony" did not, for a long time, really mean the general good of everyone there.

Today, though the majority of Americans are Christian, our Constitution and the decisions of the Supreme Court provide that as a country we profess no religion, and that citizens are guaranteed the right to adopt and practice any faith they please. Many people, however, do not understand the practical implications of the principle of freedom of religion. Widespread misunderstanding of the recent Supreme Court decision prohibiting the teaching or practice of religion in public schools has prompted some people to accuse the Court of being against religion. Further, many people believe the decision prohibits public schools from teaching *about* religion. Neither belief is accurate. The purpose of the decision is to insure that no public school student be indoctrinated in any religion. Religious instruction is neither the function nor the right of the public school. Indeed, it would infringe on the right of a child's family to encourage him to adopt their own faith or no faith at all. According to the Constitution, no public institution may influence this very personal decision.

There is ample evidence from colonial times that government sponsorship or encouragement of a particular religion can wreak havoc. In England, the Anglican Stuarts persecuted Catholics and Puritans, harassing and jailing them, fining and whipping them, and even marking their faces with brands. The Puritans under Cromwell similarly mistreated Anglicans and Catholics. James II showed favoritism to Catholics. And during all this intra-Christian persecution, the Jews were perpetual victims of prejudice and discrimination. Religious rights were guaranteed only to the sect in political ascendancy, and struggles for freedom from persecution were inevitably followed by violation of the rights of others.

One would think that the problems of the Separatists have little relevance to the problems of modern Americans. But the church-state controversy is again being bitterly debated, and we can learn from history to avoid repeating past mistakes. The Separatists did not want to belong to the Church of England, the state church, and were punished and finally forced to leave the country in order to worship as they pleased. The Pilgrims found that they could not attract new immigrants to

Plymouth because they imposed their religious beliefs on new colonists. And as recently as this century, Catholic immigrants felt compelled to open parochial schools for their children because Protestant theology was compulsory in the public school curriculum. Today the Supreme Court is called "Godless" and Catholics and Protestants still occasionally accuse each other of trying to take over the country. And secularists and other minorities are still finding it necessary to appeal to the courts to protect their rights of worship and dissent. We cannot but conclude that the framers of the Constitution were sensible in providing for government protection of religious freedom, and that the recent court decision is in keeping with a principle which history has proven wise.

However, teaching *about* religion is a legitimate function of the public schools, because the goal of the school is to disseminate knowledge and encourage independent thinking. Religion is a fact of human life and must, like other facts of life, be understood. Understanding of much of history, literature and current events requires a familiarity with the beliefs and practices of the different religions. Also, we must discuss religion openly in the schools to prevent children from developing misconceptions and prejudices about members of other religions. We need not be reminded of what happened in a modern, technologically advanced country where six million Jews were killed when fear and frustration were manipulated to transform misconceptions about Jews into murderous rage.

The high birthrate in the American colonies may be compared with the present rapid rate of growth of the world population. We are concerned with running out of adequate food and space for all the earth's people, but the colonists had no such problem. Families were large and were generally adequately provided for. Interesting here is the opinion of a visiting Englishman, quoted in the reference text, that the high birthrate was a plot against England, to provide fighting rebels. It might be useful to point out the parallel between this comment and the suspicion of many Americans in the nineteenth century that the birthrate in Catholic families was a plot to take over the government.

The reference textbook includes a page of photographs under the caption *European Influence in America*. One of the pictures shows the colorful designs characteristic of Pennsylvania Dutch art. It might be valuable to discuss, in connection with the religious history of the colonies, the dispute modern Pennsylvania Dutch people are having with local authorities over their refusal to send their children to a new consolidated high school. The Dutch do not want their children to attend a "worldly" school and absorb knowledge that would "spoil" them. They believe an eighth-grade education, by local teachers, to be adequate for the life they lead. The public school authorities maintain that these teachers are not qualified, and that the private school does not offer all of the facilities to which the children are entitled by law. Some of the Pennsylvania Dutch people have talked of emigrating to Canada, because they feel they are being unfairly treated. When a religious minority threatens to emigrate because of persecution, we are obligated to think very seriously about the problem. Who is to decide what the children need? This is not an easy question, but discussion of it may emphasize the importance and subtlety of the principle of religious freedom.

Even today, the religion of the Indians is considered by many people to be no religion at all. The colonists, exhorted by the British geographer Hakluyt and others, believed it their duty to convert the Indians to Christianity, leading them "from darkness to light . . . from the deep pit of hell to the highest heavens." Because the Indians were not Christians, they were considered low in the scale of humanity. It might be instructive to ask how well Christians and Indians could get to know each other with a barrier of this kind between them. Such contempt, condescension and ignorance contributed greatly to the eventual outbreak of hostilities between Indians and other Americans, and left a heritage of prejudice and discrimination from which Americans still suffer today.

It is interesting to note that the Toleration Act passed in Maryland in 1649 "granted religious freedom to those who professed belief in Jesus Christ." We are accustomed to thinking we have progressed a long way since then toward religious freedom, but many Congressmen—who represent both Christians and non-Christians—speak of the United States as a Christian nation. And we have not approached the ideal of toleration which includes the agnostic and the atheist. Recently a presidential nominee declared that he did not care what a man's religion was—as long as he believed in God.

To suggest that the religious and political intolerance of the colonists may be attributed to "the times" and evaluated in terms of "another way of life" is to overlook the fact that some colonists believed in religious and political tolerance. William Penn guaranteed religious tolerance in Pennsylvania to those who believed in God, and allowed all men who owned property or paid taxes to vote. The reference text declares of Penn, "He guaranteed complete religious toleration for any person who worshipped the 'one almighty and eternal God.' " But even William Penn did not recognize that "complete religious toleration," in order to be truly "complete," must be extended to those who worship no God.

Intergroup Relations and Crime

Poverty was one of the most important among the conditions which forced the English colonists to journey to America. As is so often true among the poor, the crime rate was very high, partly out of simple need for food and clothing, partly out of anger and frustration and partly because youngsters grew up in close association with criminals in overcrowded, dilapidated neighborhoods. Many small crimes drew long prison sentences or the death penalty, often on very meager evidence. But the English poor during the eighteenth century had a way out: gathering up their families and their courage, they fled—across the ocean to a new world.

In the twentieth century, the rural poor flee from the country to the city, and the minority poor from the south to the north. But there, though conditions are usually not much better and often worse, they are forced to stay. The poverty and frustration continue unabated, and the crime rate continues to rise. No longer can the poor run to a new world. The minority poor are confined within the urban ghettos as if there were hundred-foot walls around them. It is not surprising that occasionally some do run—in desperation—through the streets of the ghetto, breaking shop windows and throwing stones at police. The surprising thing is that most minority poor do not do so, and that it happens so rarely.

An account of the trial of John Peter Zenger, a newspaper editor who criticized the governor of New York in print, and whose trial paved the way for establishment of the right of freedom of the press, provides an opportunity to discuss this often-extolled but seldom-analyzed principle. Its correlative, responsibility of the press, is almost never discussed. Yet today, responsibility of the press plays a significant part in the struggle for equality. For example, a newspaper which repeatedly identifies Negro criminals by race but does not label white criminals tends to reinforce the stereotype of Negroes as violent and criminal. Because newspapers often emphasize crime news and rarely mention ordinary law-abiding citizens, the impression conveyed to the reading public is distorted. The fact is that the overwhelming majority of Negroes, Puerto Ricans, Indians and Mexican-Americans, as well as whites, do not commit crimes. Newspapers have a responsibility to make this apparent, especially in a prejudice- and fear-ridden society.

Minorities and the Law

When James I granted charters to The London Company and The Plymouth Company to found colonies in America, he provided that the English settlers would have the same rights in the colonies that they had had in England. The rights to trial by jury and representative government were guaranteed by the charters but long ignored in practice, and this injustice later became a major cause of the Revolution. The colonists repeatedly complained that their rights were being violated by the King's men, until the colonies finally exploded in violence. Here again there is an analogy to the twentieth-century United States. We might ask our students if they know of any modern instances of guaranteed rights being withheld. Not many of us are aware of the extent to which people have been deprived of their rights in America, but the facts are quickly documented. In many parts of the country Negroes, Mexican-Americans and Indians are excluded from jury panels. In other places, they are excluded if a member of their own group is on trial, with the implicit assumption that a Negro citizen cannot judge a Negro suspect impartially. (How many Caucasians are refused the right to serve on a jury because the suspect is Caucasian?) Is it really inevitable that a Negro will side with a Negro, regardless of the facts of a case? Only whites holding the stereotype that all Negroes are alike can hold such a belief.

Most children are righteously indignant to learn that the Massachusetts Bay Colony permitted only a few of its settlers to vote. Though the town meetings were attended by most citizens, those who were not Puritans were discouraged from political dissent by the harsh Puritan attitude toward religious dissent. Quakers and Catholics were often beaten, mutilated and driven from the colony just for worshipping differently. How free could they have felt to disagree on other matters?

Most children are unaware of the fact that hundreds of thousands of Americans are still disenfranchised. Economic coercion, physical intimidation, and, until recently, the "white primary" and the poll tax (still in effect in some local elections) effectively prevent many Negro Americans from voting. The situation of Indian-Americans, too, may be reconsidered in this light. Isolated from participation in local issues by their "reservation" status, they are often similarly discouraged from participating in state and federal elections. And even when minority people do vote, they are often dismayed at the way the representatives they have helped to elect ignore their rights. Men who represented Japanese-American constituents voted in 1942 to send them to concentration camps for the duration of the war.

In many areas minority people are prevented by the political structure of the community from voting for members of their own group to represent them. Political tactics are used to keep the names of minority people off the ballot, and minority-group districts are "gerrymandered," or divided into political units in a pattern which diffuses their voting strength. In areas of the country inhabited by many people who do not speak English, literacy tests are used to exclude them from voting. People who can read and write in Spanish, and who receive information and news from Spanish-language media, are thus labelled illiterate, though they are no less informed or concerned than other Americans. Though the Civil Rights Act of 1964 provided for Federal registrars to supervise voter registration in areas where discrimination was obvious, it is clear that the Federal government does not always send registrars where they are needed. In sum, disenfranchised Americans are a part of "current events," as well as of "American history."

Some of the early colonists like Roger Williams and Anne Hutchinson fled from discriminating colonies to unsettled land, but Americans who are discriminated against today do not have this option. People run from the South to the North, and find discrimination there too. With no place left to run to, some twentieth-century Americans are engaged in protest against the *status quo*. Though few people would condemn the eighteenth-century Americans for their protest, their twentieth-century counterparts have no such unanimity of support.

"Although English law prohibited the exchange of rum or guns for pelts, the colonists . . . traded these articles for furs from the Indians." This sort of statement, unexplained, may tend to confirm the stereotypes some children have of Indians. The notion—still current—that Indians react differently to alcohol than do white people may be reinforced by the statement that it was against the law to sell rum to the Indians. There is no doubt that more recent restrictions against permitting Indian-Americans to buy liquor is based on this misconception. The chemical and psychological effects of alcohol on the human body, and the reasons why people drink excessively, are identical in all races. The suggestion that Indians are different in this respect, even wrongly inferred, must not go unchallenged.

With all the furor these days about crime and delinquency —to say nothing of the resentment aroused by civil disobedience—the statement that the colonists traded liquor and guns to the Indians *against English law* might be amplified and related to the current concern over crime, delinquency and the use of civil disobedience to dramatize injustice. What is the meaning of law to people? Is there a difference between the law under which the colonists lived and the law under which Americans live today? What moves people to break the law? What were the consequences of breaking the law in colonial times? What are the consequences today? Are there times when people are justified in breaking the law? Were the colonists justified in breaking the law? These are all questions of immediate pertinence in a society undergoing rapid change.

Minority Groups and American Civilization

There is an interesting footnote in the reference text noting that the first settlers built frame houses. But it is the log cabin, not the frame house, that has become symbolic of rugged American individualism and ingenuity. Presidents start inspiring lives in them and pioneers live in them while carving out a civilization in the wilderness. The footnote, however, indicates that it was not English colonists but Swedish settlers who first built the log cabin. How many people who still hold to the Anglo-Saxon ideal of *THE* American would be pleased to acknowledge the symbolic American log cabin as Swedish? To those who use such epithets as "dumb Swede" and "Squarehead," he is just another foreigner who has contributed nothing to the development of "American" culture!

Indians were never foreigners, though they have often been treated as if they had no right to the benefits of this country. But, as we sometimes note in passing but often forget, the Indians were in great measure responsible for the survival of the Jamestown colony. Without the food and advice they gave the colonists, the English settlers could not have lasted the first winter. How often, in teaching American history, do we note that there were Indians wiser and more able than the colonists? The Texas sheriff who maintains that Indians are "naturally" criminal, and the Arizona teacher who feels Indians cannot learn as much as whites, have not learned their history very well.

Slavery in America

In 1619, twenty Negroes arrived in Jamestown on a Dutch ship. They were not slaves, but indentured servants. Like the ancestors of many white Americans, most of them worked to pay off the cost of their passage and then became free citizens. Fifty years later, however, slavery was legalized, and Negroes became an important source of labor in the colony. In general, very little is said in American history textbooks about the feelings of enslaved people, the effect of slavery on human beings or the effects of such a history on people alive today, both black and white.

We can observe in the reference text how the attitude of the author flavors, for good or ill, the presentation of historical facts. In a section on the population increase in the colonies, the authors discuss the "involuntary immigration" of convicts, prisoners of war, orphans, vagrants, paupers and slaves. By grouping these "unwilling immigrants" together, the authors emphasize that they are discussing *people,* real people who did not want to be forced to come to this country. Some of them—

both white and black—were able eventually to buy their freedom and make a new life for themselves. But most of them, especially those from Africa, remained in bondage and saw their children suffer the same fate.

Rather than just treating slavery as a dry historical fact, we might discuss how a man feels when he is considered to be another man's property. How does he feel to see his son another man's property? What does it do to a nation to have had slavery in its past? Do white people today feel guilty about this? Is it possible that the insistence of many white people that Negroes are inferior is an attempt to justify what whites have done to black people? And how do Negroes today feel? They have waited much longer for equality than did the European colonists, and few would deny that the injustices perpetrated against them have been more trying than those the colonists suffered.

Some Negro children feel uncomfortable when slavery is discussed in their history classes. One child said she felt guilty without understanding why, as if she had done something she was ashamed of. Another felt embarrassed, as if everybody were looking at her. A young graduate student reported having similar feelings in a graduate course on race relations, but became more comfortable after discussing the problem openly and even talking about her initial reluctance to participate. I believe that this feeling is in part a result of casual recitations in history lessons of the functions, market value and status of slaves, as if slavery were an ordinary economic institution. White teachers and children often calmly discuss slavery in their history classes, without ever actually acknowledging that slavery involved kidnapping people from their homes, restraining them with chains, humiliating and often torturing them. The responses to this treatment were varied: some slaves fought, some ran, some committed suicide and some prayed. Like the Indians in their relations with the colonists, like the colonists in their relations with the English, like the Jews in their relations with the Nazis, Africans' relations with white Americans depended on the immediate situation and the personalities of the people involved. Not all the colonists, for example, fought the British; some ran to Canada and some fought on the British side. It must be made clear that there is no guilt in being kidnapped and enslaved. The Jews were slaves in

Egypt, the Christians were slaves in Rome; the guilt was not theirs, but the slaveowners'. It is likely that the Negro child feels guilty, and the white child complacent, because both think that the slaves should not have let themselves be treated as they were and should have fought to resist slavery. The fact is that many did fight, and many died. Few textbooks discuss the numerous slave rebellions, or explain how slaveowners systematically destroyed the ability of the slaves to resist. Tribesmen were separated to destroy cohesiveness; family units were separated to deprive people of hope and incentive. Slaves were forced to forget their own languages and cultures. And most suffered the physical indignity of being treated like animals, to the point of violence. Despite all this, there were many carefully organized escapes and rebellions, and many free Negroes who joined the abolition movement and fought in the Civil War. It is in such a context of objectivity that the Negro child can learn about slavery without shame or embarrassment, and can recognize that there is ample cause for pride in American Negro history.

It is unwise to permit youngsters to pass over without question or discussion a statement like, "Slavery was legalized." This statement might be discussed in conjunction with one like this: People were kidnapped from their homes, bound to each other by chains, and forced to walk to the sea, where they were crammed into airless ships' holds, often with no room to sit or lie down. For almost a month they stayed in these holds, many dying, many (chained as they were) seizing the opportunity to jump overboard and drown. In America, they were auctioned off, at public sales, to the highest bidder, and became just another piece of property.

Questions to discuss with students might be: How did the people feel? How would you feel if this happened to you? Was there something wrong with the African people that made it perfectly all right to treat them this way? How did the kidnappers feel? Did they think they were doing the right thing? When a white American bought a person, did he think he was doing the right thing? In what sense can it be "legal" to do such things? Were there white Americans who believed it was wrong to kidnap and sell people? What did they do about it? If you believed something wrong was being done to people, what would you do about it? Such questions help young people to develop empathy for the victims of slavery, and also to grow in understanding of their own feelings.

The reference text includes a series of interesting photographs depicting colonial farmers, housewives, an ironworker, and a glass blower. The student reader may easily overlook the fact that all of these activities were engaged in by the unwilling colonists as well. But they were unable to direct their own efforts or to benefit from their own labor. There were African cooks, African ironworkers and artistic African painters, glassblowers and silversmiths, proud of their work. But the African artisan could be beaten and have no recourse to the law. The African mother could be taken from her children and expect no help from the local magistrate. And the African artisan could see the credit for his own ingenuity taken by the man who owned him, and have nowhere to turn for justice.

Inter-Class Relations

One of the distinguishing features of American frontier life from the beginning was the relative insignificance of rank and class. The determining factor in this frontier attitude seems to have been the common hardships which people had to withstand together. History is full of examples of the blurring of class lines when people have common goals. Evidence in social psychology indicates that the same thing happens to racial distinctions under similar circumstances. This is an important issue for teachers to consider. Do we give young people enough of an opportunity to discover such common goals, cutting across lines of class and race? Do we, and should we, ever permit them to cut across lines of behavior and I.Q.? Many educators are convinced that we should isolate the "problem" child, separate the "gifted" and the "slow learners" and establish special schools catering to single groups. But is there not a danger of fragmenting our society until all communication among various groups ceases and our common human goals are submerged?

Human Relations and War

The situation in America during the period of rivalry between France and England can teach us much about men's propensity for killing each other and a little, perhaps, about how to reduce it. Though the new world had vast wealth in furs, agricultural and metal products—enough, in fact, to add materially to the wealth of both France and England—greed and mutual suspicion led to attempts by both sides to exterminate the other. Not only did the French use the Indians to add to their wealth while the English killed Indians to add to theirs, but the French and English began to kill each other. "Thus, when Jamestown was only six years old, it sent an expedition all the way to Acadia (Nova Scotia) to wipe out a handful of French settlers," notes the text. All the way from Jamestown in Virginia to Nova Scotia in what is now Canada! If there had been more settlers, war would probably have erupted long before 1754!

Another factor in the continuous fighting between the French and English was hostile prejudice brought from the mother countries. Trade rivalry and religious hostility between the two countries were brought to America and perpetuated from generation to generation. People have come to America from different parts of the world and have, in short order, learned our prejudices and adopted our discriminatory behavior. But even before becoming "one hundred per cent American" in this way, they already have the prejudices of their native lands. Thus, the Irish hate the English, the Germans and the French distrust each other, and everybody hates the Jews! The very universality of prejudice and discrimination has led even some people of goodwill to question the possibility of eliminating them from human personality and behavior. But before we give up on the possibility of ameliorating intergroup relations, we might reflect on the fact that never before in the history of teacher education have so many of us devoted ourselves to this problem.

The depiction of wars in school history books has probably contributed to the universal acceptance of war as a way of solving problems. How can teachers encourage their students to rational behavior, intergroup amity and judicious problem-solving if their textbooks describe wars as exciting and glorious, and warriors as adventurous heroes? It is almost incidentally that the reference text notes, "In a brief but bloody battle, both Montcalm and Wolfe lost their lives." That footnote to history is preceded by a detailed description of battle that makes the war sound like a delicious adventure.

Americans in Rebellion

A natural opportunity to relate the eighteenth century to the twentieth, and the Revolutionary War to the Negro Revolution now in progress, might be a drawing or painting depicting the violence of the Revolution, like that in the text of Americans pulling down a statue of King George III. Was this incident an example of civil disobedience? How do we feel about those demonstrators, as compared to our feelings about, for example, the people who recently linked arms around a building site and refused to let work continue until the government insured that workmen were not chosen with regard to race? Or is the painting more closely related to an urban riot, with its attendant destruction of property? Certainly, property is being destroyed in the incident, and the citizens do not look very calm and controlled.

There is a woman in the painting holding a baby. What are we to think of a woman who participates in a riot with a baby in her arms? Is she irresponsible, or is she expressing her feelings of resentment and frustration in the only way she can?

Not everyone in the picture seems to be part of the mob; some are just bystanders. Among this group are several Indians, looking very unlike the stereotype that many Americans today have of Indians. They are neither violent nor depraved-looking. On the contrary, they seem to be somewhat stoical in the face of the violence of the whites.

The one Negro in the painting, an active participant in the job of pulling down the statue, appears to be just another colonist caught up in the events of the moment. But not quite as involved, perhaps, as the white man who is carrying a flaming torch. Is he holding it for light, or is he preparing to burn down some buildings?

Most of the people in the painting are not involved in the vandalism. Some are looking on in what appears to be dismay, others seem encouraging and some are merely pensive. Can this situation be compared to some of the recent riots and vandalism we have experienced? Too often, everyone in the general area of a riot is assumed to have been part of it, while in fact only a very few have been involved.

Repression, frustration and rioting are not new on the American scene. Nor are Negroes the only Americans who have been involved in them. We read without emotion about Lord Baltimore, who acquiesced to the demands of the Maryland legislature that it be allowed to frame laws because he feared an open revolt. May we compare the equanimity with which we read about past revolts to the agitation with which we view contemporary ones? Why is the Black Power advocate, who demands that black people have a powerful voice in decision-making, viewed with horror, while the colonist who demanded the same thing for himself is honored as a patriot? How differently do we evaluate the riots of 1770 and the riots of 1963? Why the difference in our attitudes? Have our ideals changed? Is the proximity of violence more fear-producing? Were there Americans in 1770 who were as fearful and hostile toward the rioters as some Americans are today? Surely we do not believe that the principles of the Declaration of Independence should be applied only to white Americans!

Many of us are disturbed at what we consider the spread of violent means of expressing dissension in our country. If the study of American history teaches us nothing else, it can disabuse us of the notion that we are traditionally a calm people, who deal with our problems rationally. Even before the Revolution, conflicts within the colonies—over land, currency, religion, representation—were violent, and riots and disorder were not uncommon. And, for more than ten years before the Revolution, "the Colonists and the British government engaged in a dramatic war of nerves, punctuated from time to time by riots and disorder." How much more attractive and admirable these riots sound than do the riots that have occurred in several American cities in the 1960's! Perhaps, if youngsters were encouraged to admire past hostilities less and to understand both past and present violence in terms of behavioral causes and effects, they might learn to prevent future violence by resolving conflict constructively and solving human problems with reason.

16 Elementary Science—
Food Preservation

An Explanatory Note
My method in this chapter, like the preceding one, has been
to associate to the ideas in the reference text intergroup facts,
ideas and sensitivities. Since the overwhelming majority of
school texts either ignores or distorts the realities of group
relations, there is no intent here to select a particular text for
adverse criticism. Rather, the objective is to confront the
reality and proceed constructively: that is,

1. Most texts are deficient in a particular area of knowledge.
2. As teachers, we are usually compelled to make some use
of the available texts.
3. The texts can be very useful if we know how to relate
them to our intergroup needs.

Following this reasoning, even a book that presents as fact
outright lies about groups, even an author who regards certain
Americans as inherently inferior, can be valuable to the curriculum, provided the teacher knows how to help the children
to recognize what the author is trying to do and to develop skill
in dealing with bigotry. However, no such book or author has
been used as a reference text here. Instead, the selections are
illustrative of a more typical approach to textbook writing, in
which intergroup concepts are omitted completely, while
certain areas of emphasis sometimes result in fostering misconceptions.

Hunger Then and Now
Using as an example the section on "Keeping Food" in the
reference text,[1] a fourth-grade science book, let us examine the

[1] Herman and Nina Schneider, *Science Far and Near*, 2nd ed. (Boston:
D. C. Heath and Company, 1961).

possibilities of relating scientific concepts to children's lives.

The section begins with the sentence, "Too much to eat, then not enough to eat. That was how people lived a long, long time ago." The poor child must find this statement ironic, for that may be exactly how he lives right now. His feelings will probably not be expressed, out of a conviction that the teacher is concerned only with people who lived "a long, long time ago." And what of the well-fed child, who sits all year next to a child who often goes hungry, or who lives only a few blocks from people who are struggling to survive? It is important for him to know that, like the people of long ago who "ate and ate" when they caught an animal because they did not know how to preserve the meat and knew there would soon be lean times, poor people often "eat and eat" because they fear they will soon be hungry. Or they buy and buy in fearful contemplation of an immediate future when there will be no money with which to buy. The book declares that it was the Indians who lived this way. Why only the Indians? Surely this was a universal pattern before the discovery of methods of food preservation.

The text also notes that Indians dried many foods in the hot sun. Why is this practice attributed only to Indians? Europeans and Africans also dried food in the sun. Today, the United States sends many varieties of dried foods to other countries, and much of the surplus food distributed to needy families in this country is dried. Continued emphasis on Indians as they lived two hundred years ago reinforces the stereotype of the Indian as a primitive. Such material must be balanced with information about the practices of other peoples and of modern Indians to avoid encouraging a stereotype.

"If only food could be kept from spoiling! Then there would not be times of too much to eat, and times of too little," the children are told. It may be at this point in his study of science that a fourth-grader loses interest, or gets angry and fed up—because the book is lying to him! In his life there may still be times of too much to eat and times of too little. The advent of refrigeration is not as important to him as is his anxiety over the future because the past has been so uncertain. It is not refrigeration that can solve this child's problems. The root of the problem may be job discrimination against his race which forces his father to work only sporadically, and then at menial jobs. The root of the problem may be an economy which outgrows certain skills and does not retrain the men thrown out of work. The root of the problem may be the very school in which the child sits, overcrowded, understaffed and inadequately supplied, because it is an Indian school or a Negro school or a Puerto Rican school. The poverty caused by inadequate education results in "times of too little to eat," and keeping food from spoiling is *not* the essential problem.

And what of countries where millions exist on bare subsistence diets and there is not enough food available to make refrigeration necessary? Refrigeration is a marvelous invention, but there are millions of people, in the United States as well as other countries, whose concerns about food do not include the problem of how to preserve it.

Because science involves practical experimentation, the teacher of a unit on food preservation will probably help the children observe what happens when food spoils. The relevance of a child's environment to the educational process may strike us with some force in such a situation. Before a teacher engages in an experiment to spoil food, she should be very sure that there are no children in her class who have gone without breakfast or lunch, or who may go without dinner. How receptive to new knowledge will a child be if he is asked to observe food spoiling while he goes hungry?

This is not to suggest that poor children should not learn about refrigeration, but that learning should take place within the context of the child's experiences and the reality of the world around him. Ignoring that world increases the suffering child's frustration and leaves the comfortable child handicapped by ignorance and lack of sensitivity.

Refrigeration and Installment Buying

While talking in class about spoiling food, it might be valuable to examine the reasons why food spoils today. (Many children know, from sad experience, that the invention of refrigeration did not solve the problem of food spoilage.) Some children's families do not have refrigerators. Perhaps they have never been able to afford one. Many of the people who live in rural areas of the country have never even *seen* a refrigerator! In the cities, it is not unusual for children to become aware of the importance of a refrigerator only after it has been repossessed by the finance company. They may want to discuss the experience, though they do not understand the time-payment plan that may have deprived them of the refrigerator after the family had already paid more than it was worth. A current scandal are the food-freezer plans which sell freezers on exorbitant payment plans, promising to provide a three- or four-month supply of high-quality food. Usually, neither the appliance nor the food is of good quality and the food supply rarely lasts longer than five or six weeks. A child upset by such a disturbing personal experience is in no frame of mind to learn scientific concepts which seem to ignore the very meaning of his own life.

Some children may have learned about food spoilage in a way so meaningful that classroom "Experiments in Spoilage" pale into insignificance. Perhaps they have seen food spoil in their refrigerators because the electricity was turned off when there was no money to pay the bill. We must make sure that they are not taught, by implication and silence, to be ashamed of this fact. Instead they can be helped to respond to this experience by charting more secure courses for themselves. If the poor child and the economically secure child are encouraged to share their experiences, they may help each other to understand the world as it really is.

Poverty and Food Quality

Poor children have some additional knowledge about food spoilage which is directly related to their economic condition, and which most people are unaware of. It has been revealed that some food chain stores ship perishable food that has not sold in the better neighborhoods to stores in the poorer areas, where it is sold as top-quality for the same, or even higher, prices. I have heard a store manager defend this practice by insisting that the food is "just as good," even though it will not sell in "better" neighborhoods. Poor children need to learn something about the appearance of food, to help them resist this kind of exploitation. And children in "better" neighborhoods need to know about this practice, which their own relatives and friends may be indulging in. The unfairness of such a practice is usually grasped immediately by young children, while many adults do not seem to understand it.

Intergroup Relations and Food

Just as poor children never taste some foods, so children in different parts of the country and of different ethnic groups are familiar with different foods. What an opportunity to make children interested in and accepting of their own, as well as others', differences!

Some adults ridicule certain foods and feel superior to those who eat them. These foods, of course, have become for some symbols of the people who eat them, a symbol denoting the inferiority of the people associated with it. The prohibition against eating pork among most Jews and Moslems is looked on as an aberration. The science class is an appropriate place to try to understand this and other dietary prohibitions and, perhaps, to examine the possibility that they stem from ancient avoidance of foods which spoiled easily. One might speculate on the universal lag between scientific knowledge and behavior change. If the study of science is to teach children about the inevitability of change and to give them tools to cope with that change, then they must understand something about human resistance to new knowledge and change, and learn to recognize such resistance in themselves.

Science and Cooperation

The last sentence in the section reads, "Because people watched, and tried, and thought, and shared what they learned, we all eat better all through the year." In its relevance to contemporary human relations, sharing is probably the key concept in scientific progress. Scientists who publicly acknowledge awards for discovery usually make a point of saying that they built on the work of their predecessors and worked in cooperation with other scientists. Cooperative, productive human relationships on an international level may help erase war from the human range of alternatives. On an interpersonal level, good human relations may free us from the constricting need to see other people as inferior.

As teachers, we might ask ourselves how important cooperation is in the school life of the children. Children read in their textbooks that sharing has made us what we are, but is sharing really encouraged in most classrooms? Is there, in their work at school, a sharing of ideas, of skills, of materials? The pattern in most schools is actually to discourage such sharing. Emphasis is put on making children work and produce as individuals. Generally, the teacher sees only herself as the sharer of knowledge, and the children as mere receivers of what she has to offer.

Such a pattern of teacher-pupil relationships overlooks exciting possibilities for using inter-pupil cooperation in the teaching-learning process. There is evidence that students trying to teach other students may succeed where teachers fail and, in the process, educate themselves. There is evidence that children at play develop patterns of interaction and self-governing rules that are marvels of efficiency and complexity. There have been several experiments in cooperation from which children emerge more accepting of others, more sensitive to the needs of their co-workers, and more aware of the world around them. The science teacher who knows that pushing back the frontiers of knowledge is a cooperative venture can make the teaching and learning of science an adventure in good human relations.

17 Spelling—Contractions and Possessives

An Explanatory Note

I have chosen from the reference text, a fourth-grade speller,[1] the chapter on contractions and possessives, to use in demonstrating how even a lesson on the mechanical use of the apostrophe can be related to intergroup matters. The sentences quoted from exercises in this book are similar to those found in many widely-used spelling and grammar texts. Its approach to the learning of language is not atypical. What such books usually overlook is that words represent ideas, attitudes and feelings. They are symbols of life experiences. The sound of a word can strike a responsive chord deep within us (witness the diagnostic uses of word association tests). To teach children about words in a way which implies that essential meanings are not of immediate importance is to defer life itself. The way we usually teach spelling is quite consistent with the pervasive belief that school is "preparation" for life, rather than a living experience. Therefore, though the chapter heading in the text-book is *Contractions and Possessives,* my recommendation is that we broaden our scope to teach *Language and Life*.

Words and Meanings

Many of us have had the experience of listening to a speaker who used words we did not understand. How anxious and angry this makes us! How often we have accused such people of using *pedaguese* or *gobbledegook!* How often we have accused them of trying harder to impress than to communicate!

Now think of how children must feel when they are compelled to learn to spell, pronounce and write words whose dictionary meanings we may tell them but whose real meanings evade them. Bombarding a child who is just learning to read

---

[1] William Kottmeyer and Kay Ware, *Basic Goals in Spelling*, 2nd ed. (St. Louis: Webster Division, McGraw-Hill Book Company, 1964).

with words and ideas which have no relevance to his life is not only frustrating for him, but may keep him from ever learning to read.

Similarly, words and ideas collected just for the sake of teaching spelling provide little motivation to learn. We ignore an opportunity to teach something meaningful when we expose children to sentences like "The skin of a frog does not have hair." A lesson in contractions and possessives is an opportunity to present an important idea or raise a controversial question. Instead of "the skin of a frog", why not "the skin of a boy"? "The skin of a boy may be brown or pink" is a simple statement of fact which may lead to some profound thinking, for a boy is a boy and though his skin color may be of passing interest, his "boyness" is what life is all about. "The wife of the president was not with him" is an exercise in vacuity, but "The president would not hire the father of the Indian boy" might be used as a starting point for discussing employment discrimination.

Just to open a newspaper is to discover a world of *significant* contractions and possessives which can be useful not merely as spelling exercises, but also for the important ideas they convey. Casually scanning an issue of a daily newspaper, I found half a dozen important items which had illustrative contractions and possessives: (1) "One of the nation's magazines" is reported as saying that Negro actors rarely play realistic human beings in TV dramas; the opinion of Kenneth Clark, a leading Negro psychologist, is that TV encourages racism. (2) One thousand neglected children are not being provided for because the city hasn't appropriated money for their care. (3) Georgia's election of Maddox shows that most of the voters in Georgia believe in segregation. (4) The Advisory Board, which will hear the complaints of citizens against policemen, has been appointed by the mayor. (5) The owner of a house is charged with refusing to sell to a Negro family. (6) The people in the neighborhood of the University protest at being forced to give up their homes in order to make room for University expansion.

Every one of the above items is related to intergroup problems which are being discussed by a considerable segment of the community. The way these problems are treated today will determine how the children now studying possessives will have to live in fifteen years. Even more, the existence of these problems has already affected their lives. How can they be prepared to cope creatively with reality by mulling over sentences like, "Let us go to the cage of the lion"? Why should learning about words be so completely divorced from learning to think and reason and learning about what is happening?

One of the reasons why we have taught spelling this way for so many years is that we have lost some awareness of the purpose of language. We often regard language as a cue to a person's social class, as a basis for evaluating a person's acceptability, as a mark of status and prestige. We forget that the purpose of language is to communicate, to express one's feelings and ideas, and that words should be learned as they are needed for such expression. In lists, words are nothing; in ideas and thoughts, they are useful tools. Sometimes it seems as if we have not progressed very far from the New England Primer, widely used during Colonial times to teach reading and spelling. It begins, "A was an Archer, who shot at a frog; B was a Butcher, who kept a large dog; C was a Captain covered with lace." Some of the textbooks used today have about as much relevance to the life of the child who studies them as does a lace-covered captain or a frog-shooting archer. How many of us cannot see how the subject matter of this primer would interfere with a child's learning? Yet how many of us teach poor children with stories exclusively about middle-class people, Mexican-American children with stories exclusively about Anglo families or Appalachian children with stories exclusively about suburban families?

Words and Attitudes

The very way in which we use words to express our feelings and ideas indicates our attitudes toward ourselves and other people. We often use words as if a fact today were a fact forever. For example, minority children so often assume that the world their parents faced is the same world they must cope with, and their parents' failure and discouragement causes them to lower their aspirations. And some people, faced with the possibility of doing away with the neighborhood school, cling to it as if it were a requisite for good education. The neighborhood school was certainly an improvement over the single school to which children from far-flung areas had to come on foot; but the well-equipped, well-staffed, centrally-located educational facility, to which a child may be comfortably transported in twenty or twenty-five minutes, is certainly superior to the factory-like block nearer his home!

We also fall into the trap of using words as if they were facts. We label people lazy, for example, and then close our minds. We do not look for the grinding poverty that causes despair, the lack of education that causes inability to compete, feelings of unworthiness which discourage one from trying or limited opportunity caused by prejudice and discrimination. The word becomes a substitute for facts and explanations.

Language and Intergroup Relations

Most of us, when we teach spelling, not only demand that children spell words correctly, but also that they pronounce words in ways they have never done before, and use words which stand for ideas that are alien to them. This may be especially true of the child from a minority group, who often uses different pronunciations and intonations than does his teacher. It may also be true of the lower-class child whose way of thinking precludes the use of certain words. It is no small thing to ask a child to change his way of speaking. It often sounds to the child as if we are insisting that he change the very way he sees himself and his world. He hears us saying, in essence, "Your world is not acceptable, *you* are not acceptable. Before you may be accepted, you must change." Also, he feels pressures to maintain his own way of speaking which conflict with the teacher's mandate. If he tries to change, the chances are that he will be accused by his peers of affectation. He may be harassed and even hurt physically if he persists in speaking differently. But the most pressing urge not to change comes from inside himself. Lower-class children accustomed to great constraint in using the pronoun "I" are generally not easily induced to use words to describe their inner feelings or to look for the sources of their attitudes. The lower-class child who has a tendency to make short, simple, categoric statements, followed by "Right?" or "Wouldn't it?" may have difficulty changing the pattern of his speech to allow for subordinate clauses, steps of reasoning and logical conclusion.

Generally, teachers are more concerned with incorrect pronunciations and incomplete sentences, and these are the points at which change is insisted upon. The child who says to the teacher, "I can't talk to my friends that way," is stating a fact of life. Just as Spanish-speaking parents have been powerless to prevent their children's corruption of Spanish with Anglicized and English words and construction, so the school teacher will be powerless to compel a change in the everyday speech of most children. But, somehow, we must help children understand that words are tools of communication and that, in different situations, with different people, different speaking styles are necessary. Somehow we must help them see that there is nothing *wrong* with a particular way of speaking, but that we need facility in a variety of kinds of speech to function in a mobile society. "If you can't talk to your friends that way," the teacher may say, "just talk to me that way."

A group of high school students might rewrite the balcony scene from Shakespeare's *Romeo and Juliet* in their own colloquial language. A group of fourth-graders may write stories about their own lives, learning to spell words that have meaning for them, and then "translating" their stories, using words that are found in newspapers or heard on radio and television. In these ways, children can develop a feeling for the flexible, functional use of language, with no suggestion that a particular way of speaking implies inferiority. A living language produces regionalisms, colloquialisms, new words and phrases as they are needed. Many new expressions develop within more or less isolated groups, like adolescents. Sometimes they have more universal roots. To the extent that language innovations are functional, they are neither inferior nor superior, any more than the people who use them are inferior or superior.

18 Arithmetic—Seventh Grade

Arithmetic Problems
and Life Problems

Arithmetic presents many opportunities for raising questions concerning intergroup relations. Every problem that deals with such matters as how much money Mr. Edwards had left after he had paid the rent, is a possible basis for a lesson in intergroup relations. If Mr. Edwards is Negro, his rent in a rundown neighborhood may be just as high as his white counterpart's rent for a well-maintained house in a good neighborhood. And since we are talking about income, how is it that the Indian Mr. Edwards rarely manages to earn as much as the white Mr. Edwards?

If arithmetic problems are really life problems, colors are as important as figures. If Mr. Brown receives $3,630 a year, Mr. Brown's family is having some difficulty surviving in our affluent society. Maybe the class ought to consider some of the solutions to this part of the problem, as well as to the part that asks, "What is Mr. Brown's income for a month?"

The reference text,[1] a seventh-grade arithmetic book, asks, "From the London office of his company, Mr. Ames had to go to South America. He decided to go by jet transport. For the trip of 6,720 miles, the cruising speed averaged 480 miles per hour. About how many hours of actual flying time did the trip take?" This is obviously a modern, up-to-date textbook, what with jet planes and flying six thousand miles on business. But, besides computing the flying time, we might change the destination of Mr. Ames to South Africa and consider how welcome he would be there if he were brown-skinned. We might even conclude that, given the pattern of employment

[1] Guy T. Buswell, William A. Brownell and Irene Sauble, *Arithmetic We Need* (Boston: Ginn and Company, 1963).

discrimination in London, Mr. Ames was probably *not* brown-skinned!

Interrelationship of
Areas of Knowledge

A teacher might legitimately question the advisability of raising such questions when her immediate aim is to teach children arithmetic. Will such questions not divert attention from the primary goal? Will the child not find it difficult to deal with so many different kinds of questions in one lesson? The answer lies in some of the recent work done in curriculum development. Educationists (including classroom teachers) have developed new curricula which attempt to integrate many areas of knowledge. The material is presented to children in a way that makes apparent the interrelationships between subject matter areas. An idea is approached, then, not as an arithmetic problem or a fact in history, but as a life concept which must be understood in terms of all available knowledge. This kind of curriculum development is a source of core curricula and team teaching. Such methods permit a mathematics specialist, for example, to work with a social studies specialist, an art teacher and a reading specialist to develop a unit on housing in which children investigate not only the historical and artistic evolution of shelters, but also social problems associated with the need for adequate shelter. Throughout, such matters as the relationships of population to housing, ethnic group to adequate housing and site size to income are explored by means of mathematical processes. The reading specialist helps to gather and prepare materials on the subject suitable for children at different levels of reading ability.

Of course, the arithmetic teacher who must work alone will not have such easy access to material on intergroup relations. However, the social studies teachers, the library references and the intergroup agencies are available in the community. The mathematics teacher may justify the extra effort needed to make use of these resources by re-examining her fundamental professional goal and the relationship of mathematics knowledge to that goal. The function of education is essentially to enable children to live fully by equipping them intellectually and emotionally to make free choices of styles of life, values and human associations. Arithmetic, like spelling, is a tool for optimal living. Its significance lies in its meaning and usefulness for people.

Part of the teacher's function is to select the areas of knowledge, concepts and problems she thinks most important for the child to learn. When we invent a mathematics problem for children to solve, we make a choice of the aspects of life we want the problem to deal with. In the process of making those choices, the teacher might ask herself what makes the income of no-color Mr. Ames a better choice than the income of black Mr. Ames?

In the reference textbook, there is an exercise on "Reading Per Cents." The teacher could easily rewrite the thirteen sentences in the exercise to give the children the opportunity to apply per cents to meaningful life situations. Why "In the Dog Show, 24% of the dogs were Collies?" Why not "In our city, 20% of the people speak Spanish"? Why "Mr. Ames paid 6% interest on his loan"? Why not "Poor people, when they buy things on the installment plan, often pay as much as 20% interest without realizing it"?

We teachers are periodically criticized for failing to inculcate moral values in our pupils. Like most adults in our society, we have a tendency to teach values by precept: Do this. Don't do that. Be good. Be kind, and so forth. I sometimes think that children have a built-in mechanism for "tuning out" this kind of moralizing. But perhaps we can make morality somewhat more meaningful if we give children an opportunity to learn what happens to victims of immoral behavior. Perhaps, for a moment, they will be able to feel what those victims must feel.

Intergroup Relations by Analogy

Sometimes an ingenious teacher can hit on a method of developing intergroup sensitivity that arises uniquely from his knowledge of his own subject matter specialty. An example is the mathematics teacher who taught intergroup relations by analogy, using positive numbers to indicate degrees of racial acceptance and negative numbers to indicate racial prejudice. Thus, adding and subtracting positive and negative numbers results in modification of the amount of prejudice. It is not very difficult to progress from this idea to the realization that levels of prejudice vary from person to person, and even from situation to situation in the same individual. Examples of specific contributing factors symbolized by the positive and negative numbers can be drawn from the pupils' personal experiences, from the daily newspaper and from incidents in the schoolyard and the community. Thus, an unpleasant experience with an individual of another group might temporarily raise the level of prejudice (adding a negative number), while an experience which corrects a misconception can lower the level of prejudice.

The concept of sets has also been used effectively to teach intergroup relations, with children finding sets and universals in the ethnic distribution of their class, their school, their city and of the world. The point that the universal is always the total human group is a point well made.

19 High School Biology—
The Digestive System

An Explanatory Note

The information included in this chapter about the structure and function of the human digestive system was taken from the reference text,[1] a high school biology textbook. Around these biological facts I have woven a lesson plan whose perspective is somewhat different from that of the traditional high school biology course.

We might say that the traditional approach to the study of biology *looks* into the living organism; in this approach, we *move* into the organism, and then move out with it into the world where the organism lives and makes contact with others. We see the living organism not only as a discrete functioning mechanism, but also as a sentient and social person, whose structure and functions are affected by the conditions of social living.

Thus, the facts included in the lesson are both biological and social-psychological in nature. The skills to be developed by the lesson are the broad skills of living. As for the teaching method, it merely suggests that the way in which information is discovered be as relevant to the students as are the facts themselves.

I cannot resist adding a brief postscript to this chapter on biology, in the light of recent events. The transplantation of hearts, with all the attendant publicity, has raised some fascinating questions regarding intergroup relations which can be incorporated into the teaching of biology.

One of my Teacher Corps interns observed to a fifth-grade class that a "colored" man's heart had been given to a white man. Some of the children were sure that this would make the white man a Negro. Furthermore, they believed that the heart

1 James H. Otto and Albert Towle, *Modern Biology* (New York: Holt, Rinehart and Winston, 1965).

recipient's skin would gradually turn darker. "Not *very* dark," they assured the intern, because the "colored" donor was not very dark.

In addition to the children's misconceptions about the functioning of the human body, witness how their perceptions of race are determined by our social values: if a person is "part Negro," then he is a Negro, but being "part white" does not make him white. The concept of "part Negro" is reduced to absurdity when the "part" is literally a part of the body, and we can see the essential error in our racial categories.

The Digestive System: Digestion in Contemporary Society

I. General Objectives

    A. To help students understand the biological facts of the human digestive system

    B. To help them see the relationship between optimal digestive function and the social facts of life

    C. To involve them in life situations in which knowledge of biological facts can help them solve broad-based human problems

II. Specific Goals

    A. Exposure to facts and ideas

        1. Tissues cannot use most foods in their undigested form

            a. Many food substances not soluble in water

            b. Many food substances too complex chemically

        2. Digestion breaks down complex foods

            a. Mechanically

            b. Chemically

        3. Organs of the Digestive System

            a. Alimentary canal: Mouth, tongue, teeth, esophagus, stomach (gastric glands), small intestine (intestinal glands), large intestine

            b. Glands with ducts leading into digestive organs: Salivary glands, liver, pancreas

        4. Poverty results in interference with digestive functioning

            a. Loss of teeth

      b. Alcoholism

      c. Drug addiction

  5. Ignorance results in interference with digestive functioning

      a. Many people do not know that certain foods are harmful to digestive organs

      b. Many people do not know that certain digestive symptoms need medical treatment

  6. Crowdedness affects digestion

      Irritability and anger due to crowdedness interfere with digestive functioning

  7. Frustration affects digestion

      a. Causes anger

      b. Causes loss of ambition

  8. Effects of prejudice and discrimination

      a. Poverty: Result of limited vocational opportunity in getting a job, keeping a job, rising in position

      b. Ignorance: Result of inferior education, destruction of ambition, early school departure

      c. Crowded conditions: Result of limited available housing, difficulty securing housing loans

      d. Frustration: Result of feeling of helplessness in a hostile society, failure in an inferior school, feeling of inadequacy and lack of self-worth because of segregation

  9. Effects of digestive dysfunction

      a. Loss of energy

      b. Loss of ambition

      c. Anxiety

      d. Irritability

B. Development of specific skills

  1. Ability to see poverty as the cause and result of identifiable factors

  2. Ability to see human physical dysfunction as a result of social dysfunction

  3. Ability to empathize with people in different life circumstances

  4. Ability to relate meaningfully to people in different life circumstances

5. Ability to see success in life as directly related to biological functioning

C. Development of attitudes
   1. Abandoning the view that poor people are immoral, with the implication that if they lived "right" they would not be poor
   2. Accepting people of all groups as members of the same biological club

III. The Learning Process
   A. Motivation
      1. Start with a question to which all the students are able to respond in some way, like, "Who had breakfast this morning?" Such a question involves every student in the discussion. Those who have eaten recently may be interested in what has happened to the food. Those who are hungry—and can hear their stomachs growling—may be interested in knowing the cause of such noises.
      2. Encourage the students to raise questions relating to the structure and function of the digestive system, and the relationship of that system to human social functioning. The teacher might begin by asking such questions as, "Who has a toothache right now? Who has ever had a toothache?"
      3. Hand out cookies or some other treat and ask for observations on what the teeth and tongue do in chewing and what else happens to the food inside the mouth.
      4. Show the students the rest of the cookies and say that you have enough to give each person another one, but that you will not do so. Encourage them to describe how they feel about wanting (needing) the food and being unable to get it.
      5. Tell the students that they must stay in school until midnight for a special experiment. No food will be available until they get home. After they have expressed anger, suffering or annoyance, tell them that they may have a chemical which will make their

anger and frustration disappear temporarily. The chemical's only drawback is that it may be habit-forming and may cause tissue destruction if used for a prolonged period of time. Ask how many would like to take some. Elicit explanations of the reasons why some say yes and some say no.

B. Activities

1. Identify individuals and groups interested in particular areas of the discussion.
2. Students interested in teeth may collect extracted teeth from local dentists and fix them in plaster to illustrate the different types of teeth and their functions. They may, in the process, be guided to find out which population groups visit dentists regularly and which do not.
3. A group interested in hunger may interview local anti-poverty and welfare officials to gather facts about hunger in the community. (They may get somewhat different perspectives from local civil rights agencies.)
4. Some people may want to observe their own feelings and behavior while very hungry and to compare them with their responses when well-fed to such situations as: taking a written test; remembering lists of numbers; trying to convince someone of one's own point of view; playing basketball; listening to a lecture, and discussing feelings about life.
5. The next step might be to combine activities 2 and 3, to attempt to understand the feelings of people who are chronically hungry. Role-playing would be a valuable aid, with students taking the part of hungry people in a variety of life situations, like paying attention in class or working at a job, with the parts of teacher and employer played by students as well.
6. Some people may want to trace the changes in a piece of food: one may prefer to read about the subject; another may want to use mechanical and chemical processes to simulate digestion; a third

may be interested in determining what happens when one or another process is inefficient. (Perhaps three such people can work together as a group, learning to relate effectively to each other, sharing information and experiences and helping each other to research, clarify and synthesize.)

7. Perhaps the head of a local hospital clinic may be interested in sharing with the students medical data on diseases in the community associated with digestive dysfunction related to poverty, ignorance, crowded conditions and frustration.

8. Students may be encouraged to devote some time each week volunteering their services to one of the agencies with which they have become familiar during their investigation of "Digestion in Contemporary Society." Perhaps they can begin to see a place for themselves in helping disadvantaged people. If the students themselves are poor or rejected because of minority-group membership, they may begin to see some hope and direction for themselves by becoming actively involved in changing their own lives.

20 Anthologies for Children

Secondary Poetry and Prose

Much of what is most beautiful and valuable about different nations and ethnic groups is expressed in the work of their writers. Unfortunately, most publishers of literature textbooks and school anthologies ignore this opportunity to teach children about other groups. In fact, the selections they make often serve to perpetuate the stereotypes we hope to eliminate in intergroup education. Often, too, the selections touch wounds which neither publishers nor teachers are aware of, and cause the children who read them pain and anxiety.

A startling example, especially for those of us who have long loved the Romantic poets, is William Blake's "The Little Black Boy," which is included in a recent senior high-school poetry anthology.[1] Though the accompanying notes assure readers that the poem does not concern racial discrimination since "at the time when it was written . . . there was no racial tension," the poem does reflect Blake's white-oriented value system. His poem may be about transcendent love and the burdens of mortality, and there may have been no overt racial tension in England in 1789, but Blake—like most contemporary whites—betrays his "white is right" philosophy:

> My mother bore me in the southern wild,
> And I am black, but O! my soul is white;
> White as an angel is the English child,
> But I am black, as if bereaved of light.

Angels are white, souls are white, and being black is bereavement. How different is this from what our colored citizens hear today? Of all the poems in the English language, why select this one as an exercise in understanding love?

[1] Clice C. Coleman and John R. Theobald, eds., *An Anthology Introducing Poetry* (New York: Holt, Rinehart, and Winston, 1964), p. 362.

Why not include instead the poem "As I Grew Older" by the Negro poet, Langston Hughes? He also speaks of a transcendent emotion, but for him it is not love. The poem is a cry of disappointment and disillusionment. Such a poem speaks directly to minority children whose massive disappointment affects their perceptions of self and limits their motivation to succeed. It also speaks to majority children who see brown-skinned people only from a psychological distance. It acquaints them with a fact of life that they have had no other opportunity to learn:

> It was a long time ago.
> I have almost forgotten my dream.
> But it was there then,
> In front of me,
> Bright like a sun—
> My dream.
>
> And then the wall rose,
> Rose slowly,
> Slowly,
> Between me and my dream.
> Rose slowly, slowly,
> Dimming,
> Hiding,
> The light of my dream.
> Rose until it touched the sky—
> The wall.
>
> Shadow.
> I am black.[2]
>
> I lie down in the shadow.
> No longer the light of my dream before me,
> Above me.
> Only the thick wall.
> Only the shadow.
>
> My hands!
> My dark hands!
> Break through the wall!
> Find my dream!

2 From James Weldon Johnson, ed., *The Book of American Negro Poetry* (New York: Harcourt, Brace and Company, 1931), pp. 240–241.

> Help me to shatter this darkness,
> To smash this night,
> To break this shadow
> Into a thousand lights of sun,
> Into a thousand whirling dreams
> Of sun!

Anthology after anthology includes only the spirituals of slave days as examples of "poetry" by Negroes. And usually the songs selected are those that seem to reaffirm the traditional white man's notion of the docile, easy-going Negro whose brightest wish was an eternity in Heaven. There is evidence that "Swing Low, Sweet Chariot" and "Steal Away" may actually have been texts approved and insisted upon by white slave-masters because they made slaves more accepting of their lot. The chances are, however, that the songs sung by the slaves when whites were not present recounted their feelings and aspirations much more accurately. But these songs do not find their way into high school anthologies.

If spirituals must be selected as examples of Negro poetry, even the song

> Go down, Moses
>   'Way down in Egypt land,
> Tell ole Pharaoh,
>   Let my people go

offers more insight into the Negro people and their situation at the time when spirituals were born. At least it can serve as an introduction to a discussion about how slaves really felt about their lives, and some of the things they did to change them. At least part of the appreciation of poetry involves an appreciation of the people who gave birth to it.

Some more recent Negro writers have marvelled at the ability of their ancestors to bring such beauty out of such pain. James Weldon Johnson was one of those who perpetuated the tradition of religion and song in his own writings. But the high school anthologist prefers to see in Johnson's poetry only the safe subject of religion and to ignore the pride of heritage that might give strength to some young contemporary reader. Why else would an anthologist select the one poem of Johnson's that does nothing but repeat the story of Genesis? It is true that the imagery is impressive, and I do not mean to suggest that every poem in an anthology must deal with immediate reality. However, the pattern in many anthologies seems generally to be to avoid reality altogether. Certainly, the reality of intergroup relations is almost never mentioned.

Perhaps, if only spirituals and religious poems must be chosen, the selection from James Weldon Johnson might be a poem which moves beyond the spiritual to a commentary on it, and on the wondrous facility of the oppressed man to sing in beauty. His "O Black and Unknown Bards" is a paean to the man who, "though still about his hands he felt his chains," could breathe a "comforting, melodic sigh."

> What merely living clod, what captive thing,
> Could up toward God through all its darkness grope,
> And find within its deadened heart to sing
> These songs of sorrow, love and faith, and hope?
> How did it catch that subtle undertone,
> That note in music heard not with the ears?
> How sound the elusive reed so seldom blown,
> Which stirs the soul or melts the heart to tears.[3]

One colorfully illustrated junior high school anthology[4] devotes a double page to odes to parents. On one side is a poem about fathers, illustrated with a sketch of a white father. On the other side is the following poem about a white mother:

> My mother's face is clear as the sun,
> Her eyes like brown brook water.
> Her hands are cool as shadowy moss,
> Her voice is low with laughter.
>
> My mother, watching the talking trees
> And the scud of clouds on the sky,
> Knows when to hang our bright clothes out
> For the morning wind to dry.
>
> She knows when to plant her garden seeds,
> And when to gather apples

[3] From *Saint Peter Relates an Incident* by James Weldon Johnson. Copyright 1917, 1921, 1935 by James Weldon Johnson, © 1963 by Grace Nail Johnson. Reprinted by permission of The Viking Press, Inc.
[4] Paul Witty, Miriam E. Peterson and Alfred E. Parker, *Reading Roundup*, Book One (Boston: D. C. Heath, 1958), p. 25.

And wild blueberries for sweet hot pies,
And when to expect dark dapples

Of mud on faces and hands, and scratches
On children's bare brown knees,
My mother's weather vane is her heart
And the lean of her dooryard trees.[5]

This is a pallid picture of a mother from some never-never land of children's textbooks, but perhaps it has meaning for some children. There is no point in evaluating the quality of the poetry, though one cannot help wondering why such vapidity is selected from all the thousands of words written about mothers!

But even this poem might be useful if it were printed side by side with Langston Hughes's "Mother to Son":

Well, son, I'll tell you:
Life for me ain't been no crystal stair.
It's had tacks in it,
And splinters,
And boards torn up,
And places with no carpet on the floor—
Bare.

But all the time
I'se been a-climbin' on,
And reachin' landin's,
And turnin' corners,
And sometimes goin' in the dark
Where there ain't been no light.
So boy, don't you turn back.
Don't you set down on the steps
'Cause you finds it's kinder hard.
Don't you fall now—
For I'se still goin', honey,
I'se still climbin'
And life for me ain't been no crystal stair.[6]

Perhaps the child can learn from a comparison of the two poems that there is a difference between his point of view and

[5] From *The Little Whistler* by Frances Frost. Copyright 1949 by McGraw-Hill, Inc. Used by permission of the McGraw-Hill Book Company.

[6] Arna Bontemps, ed., *American Negro Poetry* (New York: Hill and Wang, 1963), p. 67.

his mother's. Somewhere the child must discover that his omniscient and omnipotent mother is, in reality, struggling to survive. Somewhere he must learn that he cannot see the world only from his own point of view.

Perhaps, because of the realities of his own life, one child who reads the first poem may see nothing in it but another meaningless school exercise. But perhaps another child reading the second poem may suddenly become aware of a world different from his own warm safe one.

When we maintain comfortable fictions about saintly motherhood and innocent childhood we are doing our children a disservice. Such fictions and stereotypes cater to our own comforts, not the childrens'. Children see and hear accurately what is going on around them, but their understanding is limited. The fictions that we present to them as fact merely confuse and frighten them. Ultimately, this confusion and fear can result in the kind of rebellion we are witnessing today, which mocks and discards all adult values as lies and regards anyone over thirty years of age as the enemy.

I recently heard a principal rebuke a young teacher for permitting his Negro twelfth-graders to read certain writings by Negro authors. He objected to the selections on the grounds that they made the youngsters angry at whites. "But," protested the teacher, "these are the works of major writers. You're objecting to Richard Wright and James Baldwin." But the principal was willing to forego the opportunity to permit the students to appreciate first-rate writing because he was afraid. He made the common error of thinking that expressing anger or hearing it expressed actually causes that anger.

The children in the principal's school probably *were* hostile to whites. But James Baldwin did not cause the anger. They were angry about a great many unjust things that were happening to them over which they had no control. Reading Baldwin may actually have helped them in a number of ways. For one thing, they might at last have learned to give words to the anger and disappointment that corroded their spirits. Most of us have had the almost healing experience of recognizing in a great writer's words our own unexpressed feelings. Some of the frustration of struggling with those feelings has been eased by recognizing that better men than we have similarly struggled.

Furthermore, if the students had been allowed to read Baldwin and Wright, they might have revised their opinion of school. School might no longer have seemed a "jail," as one of the boys put it, but instead a place where the spirit can be truly free. The right to have feelings, to express them and to examine them is the real meaning of human freedom. But if our strongest feelings are denied recognition in school, then school is little more than a jail.

When Richard Wright says,

> I am nobody
> A red sinking autumn sun
> Took my name away[7]

he is saying what thousands of children feel and are unable to put into words. James Baldwin's feelings of fear and self-hatred also strike a responsive chord in children who may never become writers, but who need such self-awareness to fulfill their birthright as human beings.

> What was most difficult was the fact that I was forced to admit something I had always hidden from myself, which the American Negro has had to hide from himself as the price of public progress; that I hated and feared white people. This did not mean I loved black people; on the contrary, I despised them, possibly because they failed to produce Rembrandt. In effect, I hated and feared the world. And this meant, not only that I thus gave the world an altogether murderous power over me, but also that in such a self-destroying limbo I could never hope to write.[8]

Elementary Readers

In this era of growing demand for multi-ethnic reading material, teachers must beware of the readers and anthologies that fulfill the letter of the requirements but lack meaningful substance. Some publishers of elementary readers, for example, retain old texts and concepts, but occasionally include a brown face in the illustrations. Some high school anthologies, in superficial recognition of minority participation in American life and letters, contain a short account of the life of, say,

---

7 Bontemps, p. 104. Copyright by Mrs. Ellen Wright.

8 James Baldwin, *Notes of a Native Son* (Boston: Beacon Press, 1955). Reprinted by permission of the Beacon Press, copyright © 1955 by James Baldwin.

Althea Gibson. Such patchwork concessions do not fill the gaps in knowledge we have noted earlier. They are, in at least one way, more dangerous than the complete omission of all non-white-Anglo-Saxon material. Such symbolic gestures can delude us into believing that we are providing what is necessary for the children's education in intergroup relations, and keep us from doing more.

On the other hand, a story like "Meet Miki Takino," published in a first grade reader,[9] is a charming example of how a child may be entertained and taught something significant at the same time. The story, with its simple acceptance of people of different races, blurs the racial divisions among us and reaches beyond them to universal human needs. But it does this without ignoring race or pretending that it does not exist. In the story, a small boy of Japanese ancestry asks a number of Caucasian adults to be his grandparents, because his own are no longer living. The adults accept with delight, touched by the small boy's need.

Of course, the teacher must expand this experience for her young readers by raising the question of whether whites can be grandparents to Orientals—that is, if the children do not raise the question first. "If you needed a grandfather in a hurry, would you ask Mr. Kiuchi, the grocer, to be your grandfather?" "If you were in Miki's place, would you ask Mrs. Smith, the flower dealer, to be your grandmother?" Just how *do* the children feel about this crossing over of the races?

We must bear in mind that this story may be more meaningful to California children than to children from New York. It may be quite easy for children on the East Coast to accept close relationships between Orientals and whites, because there is little opportunity for such relationships in their lives. Prejudices have not come to the surface, and they can still maintain with considerable honesty that they feel no animosity toward each other. If children in New York are given this story to read, the meaning of the experience may be extended by role-playing the various parts and by changing the race of Miki and his parents to Negro. This situation is more realistically applicable to their lives, and will tend to bring out into the open their real feelings about each other.

[9] Helen M. Robinson and others, *Wide Horizons,* Book One (Chicago: Scott, Foresman and Company, 1966), pp. 56–90.

Using whimsy to make lessons in intergroup relations palatable is another snare that publishers, and teachers, sometimes fall into. We have all met animals who speak like people, hens who predict the sky is falling and the ant who is a model of industry and prudence. I have always felt that the delight that adults feel in animal stories is just that—an adult delight, fed on hazy memories of an idyllic childhood. I think children appreciate stories about people much more than they do those about anthropomorphic elephants. Be that as it may, it seems unwise to depend on animal stories to help children develop concepts of human behavior (to say nothing of the errors we perpetuate about *animal* behavior!). The child may read about brown bunny rabbits and white bunny rabbits with interest and pleasure, but there is no evidence that he will be as accepting of brown people or white people as he is of bunny rabbits. This is reminiscent of the young boy whose father spent some time explaining to him the intricacies of the relationships between male birds and female birds and male bees and female bees. The boy was fascinated with the account. Some years later, however, the family doctor was compelled to teach him the intricacies of the relationships between men and women.

There is a wealth of good literature, in English and in translation, that can be offered to children to make them freer, broader human beings. It is amazing, however, to see the many anthologies that offer young readers nothing but the pale and the bland. We seem sometimes to be trying to make sure that young people never get any kicks from anything that goes on in school.

V "Let's add it to the course of study"

Once a subject has been added to the standard curriculum of a school system, it is draped with a mantle of respectability that almost precludes doubt about whether or not it ought to be taught. The subject has the approval of the administration, and such approval implies that the school authorities have assumed the responsibility of dealing with objections from parents, principals and teachers. It is thus usually the school system that takes the lead in broadening the curriculum, and stands ready to absorb the initial shocks of social change.

Many teachers who would, I think, like to teach Intergroup Relations, hesitate to be the innovators themselves, and to assume all the attendant risks. When Intergroup Relations becomes an official part of the curriculum, the risks are institutionalized, and the individual teacher is freed to deal creatively with problems of resistance as they arise.

It must be emphasized that a single unit in Intergroup Relations does not provide all that is needed. There is always the danger that such a unit will become a substitute for permitting children to discover intergroup knowledge and develop sensitivity to the intergroup implications of every subject matter area. However, for the official support and initial guideline it offers to the teacher, the inclusion of such a unit in the standard curriculum can make a significant change in teaching content, method and over-all philosophy.

21   Starting a Unit in Intergroup Relations—First Grade

An Explanatory Note

This unit is designed for a class made up of white, Anglo children. However, the knowledgeable and sensitive teacher will undoubtedly see possibilities for using it in a desegregated situation or one in which all the children are of the same minority group.

Goal and Purposes

The single fundamental goal of teaching a unit like this is to give the child an opportunity to broaden his experience of people. The chances are that his life experiences center around his own group, and that his perception of himself as well as his responses to others are colored by ethnocentricity. As he begins, both vicariously and in reality, to interact with people from other groups, the child will unavoidably correct his own misconceptions about others and about his own group, and will develop an increasing capacity for objectivity.

The Initial Experience

Children like to hear stories, so the teacher might begin by telling them a story:

> "Once upon a time—last week, in fact—there were two boys. One was named Jimmy and one was named Timmy. Jimmy and Timmy had never met. Jimmy lived in ____(the white section of your city). Timmy lived in ____(the colored section of your city). Jimmy had blond hair and brown eyes. Timmy had brown eyes, too, and brown skin. They were both six years old.
>
> Timmy's mother worked in (the white section). She decided that she would enroll Timmy in ____(your

school), so that he would be near where she worked and she could pick him up each day after school.

The principal welcomed Timmy to his new school, and brought him to the first grade class. Timmy was introduced to Miss Smith, the teacher. Miss Smith smiled at him and said, "How do you do, Timmy? We're happy to have you join us. Sit down here, in the empty seat by Jimmy. We are all learning about sets."

Timmy sat down, and Miss Smith went on with the lesson.

Identifying with the Characters

When you have finished the story, ask the children the kinds of questions we usually ask ourselves when we read:

> "How do you think Timmy felt?"
> "How would you feel if you were Jimmy?"
> "How did Miss Smith feel?"
> "How did Timmy's mother feel?"

(Be sparing with words in your questions, lest you reveal to the children your own feelings or your convictions about how they *ought* to feel.)

Often one child will seem to identify closely with a particular character in the story. He will seem to "know" just how the character feels; he may even reveal some of his own feelings and indicate that they are the same as the character's. Say to this child, "You seem to know how Timmy feels. Pretend that *you* are Timmy." To another child say, "Pretend that you are Jimmy."

Setting the Scene for Role-Playing

"Now, let us imagine that the class is over. Everybody is out on the playground. You, Jimmy, go down the slide just as Timmy is running by, and you bump into each other."

As you set the scene, place the children in the appropriate positions, either in front of the room or in the center of a circle of chairs. Permit the role-players and the spectators to help set the scene and decide on the props.

When the scene is set, remind everybody that Timmy (colored) and Jimmy (white) have just collided. Then say, "Show us what happens now."

Observing the Interaction

As the children act out the scene, look for expressions of anti-Negro feeling, as well as attitudes of rejection of outsiders and newcomers. Look also for some conscious recognition on the part of the child playing the Negro that the white child has such feelings.

When the scene comes to a natural close, ask each role-player how he felt about what happened. Then give the observers a chance to react to what they have seen. You might ask, "How do you think Jimmy felt about the new boy? What did he do (or say) that makes you think that?" "How do you think Timmy felt when Jimmy said, 'You don't belong here.'"

Do not admonish any child for his feelings or behavior. Free them, for once, from adult approval or disapproval and give them an opportunity to bring into the open what is inside them.

Changing the Pattern of Interaction

During the general discussion, some of the children who watched the scene may indicate that they think the incident would have happened differently. If you get no such clues, you might ask, "Would anyone have said something else after the collision, or acted in another way?"

Permit the children to act the scene a number of times with different participants. In the general discussion, help the children to see how a person's behavior calls forth certain responses from others, and how a change in behavior elicits a change in response.

Broadening the Scope of the Experience

Set another scene, in which Timmy tells his mother what has happened in school. Watch to see if the children have a realistic perception of a Negro mother's feeling and behavior. Do they act the part completely unrealistically, or is Timmy's mother very much like their own mothers?

How about a scene between Jimmy and his mother? Does the white mother warn her child about Negroes? Are the children's misconceptions, fears and hostilities apparent in the words they put in Jimmy's mother's mouth?

Adding Experiences

In the general discussion which should follow the performance of the different scenes, you may begin to raise questions (if the children do not) which will involve:

1. discussion with their own parents

2. searching out facts in books

3. meeting Negro adults

4. visiting all-Negro schools and meeting Negro children

5. working cooperatively with Negro children

The children should be given time—before and after these experiences—to discuss freely how they feel and what they think, until the discomfort of talking about race disappears (for the teacher as well as the children).

The following are samples of questions which might be raised to encourage further activities:

1. In our play, Jimmy's mother did not want him to play with Timmy because Timmy was colored. How do you think your mother would feel about this? Why don't you ask her?

2. Timmy had an aunt who thought all white people disliked Negro people. Do all the white people you know dislike Negro people? How do you know? Have you ever talked to them about this? Why don't you?

3. Jimmy told his mother that Timmy was good at athletics, and his mother answered that colored people usually are. How can we find out if colored people are better at athletics than white people?

4. Jimmy's mother told him to invite Timmy to lunch. Jimmy said he didn't know what colored children ate for lunch. Do colored and white children eat different things? How can we find out?

5. Timmy's father in our play is a doctor. Is your doctor colored or white? Would you like to meet a colored doctor?

6. Have you ever played with colored children? Would you like to? What games would you like to play? Would you like to have lunch together?

7. Would you like to have children from ____(a Negro school) work together with us on the Thanksgiving mural? On the history play?

If there is an opaque or transparency projector available, you may be able to use these suggestions:

1. "I have some pictures of Negro and white children working and playing together in school. Would you like to see them?"

2. "I have pictures of Roy and his family. Roy is a boy I know who is colored. He is in the first grade in (another city). He has a sister and a baby brother. His father is a school teacher. Would you like to see the pictures?"

3. "Look through the magazines and newspapers at home and bring any pictures of Negro people you find. We'll put them on the bulletin board (or around the room). What kind of work do these people do? This man looks like a teacher, this one like a doctor. Let's write what they do under the picture."

4. Find a picture that has five or more Negro and Caucasian individuals in it, perhaps in different types of dress (coveralls, formal clothes, etc.) in a recognizable setting (in a school yard, on a bus, etc.). The picture should not indicate what is going on, but should lead one to speculate on what *may* be happening. Flash it on the wall and encourage the children to say what they think is happening. Their stories will indicate their feelings, perceptions and misconceptions about Negroes and Negro-white relations, and will provide clues about what they need to be taught. In addition, the children will have had the opportunity to share their perceptions, and perhaps to correct some of their errors, in the course of the discussions.

5. First graders love to "write" their own stories. After they have had some interracial experiences, let them describe them, while you write the words on the board. Compiling

the stories into a book can be an exciting culmination for the unit. Here are some topics you may use:

>My First Colored Friend
>Jamie Smith (one of the colored children met in the other school)
>I Never Knew Until Now
>How Surprised I Was!
>It Gave Me A Good Feeling
>Never Again!
>The Visit

6. Provide brown as well as white-skinned dolls for use during free playtime.
7. Books, movies and film strips on intergroup relations are available in public libraries and in the collections of local intergroup agencies and may be borrowed for use in the classroom.

Suggested Readings

This bibliography is far from a complete one of the materials in Intergroup Relations that teachers will find useful. Nor does it list the many books and articles published in the past twenty years that laid the foundations for current thinking in the field. It merely offers a selection or two in several categories that the teacher can put to immediate use in preparing her lessons. Leaders like Hilda Taba, Lloyd Allen and Elaine Cook, William Van Til, Arnold Rose, Dan W. Dodson, Goodwin Watson and William Heard Kilpatrick are not all represented here, but each reference leads to these and others who have made significant contributions.

Allport, Gordon W. *The Nature of Prejudice*. Boston: The Beacon Press, 1954. 537 pages.
(The classic analysis of a pervasive factor in human personality.)

Alpenfels, Ethel. *Sense and Nonsense About Race*. New York: Friendship Press, 1957. 64 pages.
(Informational presentation by an anthropologist of scientific data that explodes myths.)

Brace, C. L. and M. F. Ashley Montagu. *Man's Evolution*. New York: The Macmillan Company, 1965. 352 pages.
(A readable and scientific explanation of human differences.)

Clark, Kenneth B. *Dark Ghetto*. New York: Harper and Row, 1965. 253 pages.
(An "involved observer's" account of the problems of ghetto communities.)

Clark, Kenneth B. *Prejudice and Your Child,* second edition and enlarged. Boston: The Beacon Press, 1963, 247 pages.
(An answer to those who think children are not concerned with race.)

Dean, John P. and Alex Rosen. *A Manual of Intergroup Relations*. Chicago: The University of Chicago Press, 1955. 194 pages.

(Practical recommendations for organizations working to improve intergroup relations.)

Epstein, Charlotte. *Intergroup Relations for Police Officers*. Baltimore: Williams and Wilkins, 1962. 194 pages.
(What police officers—and other professionals—need to know about police-minority relations and the function of democratic law.)

Federal Interdepartmental Committee on Children and Youth. *When the Migrant Families Come Again—A Guide for Better Community Living*. Washington: U.S. Government Printing Office, January, 1955. 25 pages.
(How different communities helped themselves by improving relations with migrant families.)

Franklin, John Hope. *From Slavery to Freedom: A History of American Negroes,* second edition, revised and enlarged. New York: A. A. Knopf, 1956. 622 pages.
(An excellent survey of Negro history.)

Giles, H. Harry. *The Integrated Classroom*. New York: Basic Books, Inc., 1959. 338 pages.
(An account of experiences with desegregation, suggestions for lessons, bibliography and list of resources for teachers.)

Goodman, Mary Ellen. *Race Awareness in Young Children*. New York: Collier Books, 1964. 351 pages.
(From the author's introduction: "There are offered here some inventories of the thoughts and feelings of young children, brown and white, and some evidence concerning the background hows and whys.")

Katz, William Loren. *Teacher's Guide to American Negro History*. Anti-Defamation League of B'nai B'rith, 315 Lexington Avenue, New York, New York 10016. 1968. 192 pages.

Kibbe, Pauline R. *Latin Americans in Texas*. Albuquerque: University of New Mexico Press, 1946. 302 pages.
(Though focused on Texas, the problems dealt with are problems of Latin Americans anywhere in the United States.)

Kozol, Jonathan. *Death At An Early Age*. Boston: Houghton Mifflin Company, 1967. 240 pages.
(Subtitle: The Destruction of the Hearts and Minds of Negro Children in the Boston Public Schools.)

McNickle, D'Arcy and Harold E. Fey. *Indians and Other Americans; Two Ways of Life Meet*. New York: Harper and Row, 1959. 220 pages.
(A chronicle of injustices perpetrated on Indian Americans.)

Montagu, M. F. Ashley. *Man's Most Dangerous Myth; The Fallacy of Race,* revised edition. New York: Columbia University Press, 1945. 304 pages.
(Information on the idea of race.)

Montagu, M. F. Ashley. *On Being Human.* New York: Henry Schuman, 1966. 128 pages.
(The history of the development of the human race proves that it is human nature to cooperate.)

Myrdal, Gunnar, with Richard Sterner and Arnold Rose. *An American Dilemma,* paperback, 2 volumes. New York: McGraw-Hill Book Company, 1964. 1330 pages.
(The most comprehensive collection to date of the available knowledge in race relations in the United States.)

Noar, Gertrude. *The Teacher and Integration.* Washington: National Education Association, 1966. 99 pages.
(An attempt to make the teacher aware of and sensitive to intergroup problems as they are manifested in the classroom.)

Our Greatest Challenge. Human Relations Guide to Intergroup Education in Schools. Harrisburg: Pennsylvania Department of Public Instruction, 1962. 57 pages.
(Specific suggestions for incorporating intergroup teachings into the standard curriculum.)

Racial Isolation in the Public Schools, A Report of the U.S. Commission on Civil Rights. Washington: Government Printing Office, 1967. Volume I, 276 pages; Volume II, 293 pages.
(Discusses, among other things, . . . "the relationship between racially isolated education and the outcomes of that education, and the impact of racial isolation on the attitudes and interracial associations of Negroes and whites . . .".)

Report of the National Advisory Commission on Civil Disorders. New York: Bantam Books, 1968. 608 pages plus charts and pictures.
(An analysis of racial disorders in 1967 and recommendations for preventing future disorders.)

Reissman, Frank. *The Culturally Deprived Child.* New York: Harper and Row, 1962. 140 pages.
(Stresses the strengths of the poor child that the effective teacher can utilize in the classroom.)

Saenger, Gerhart. *The Social Psychology of Prejudice.* New York: Harper and Brothers, 1953. 304 pages.
(The nature of prejudice and discrimination and their manifestations.)

Senior, Clarence. *The Puerto Ricans: Strangers—Then Neighbors.* Chicago: Quadrangle Books in cooperation with the Anti-Defamation League of B'nai B'rith, 1961. 128 pages.
(An account of problems faced by Puerto Ricans on the mainland and progress made toward solving them.)

Shaftel, George and Fannie R. *Role-Playing for Social Values: Decision-Making in the Social Studies.* Englewood Cliffs, New Jersey: Prentice-Hall, 1967. 431 pages.
(The rationale and technique of role-playing and materials for use in the classroom.)

Silberman, Charles E. *Crisis in Black and White.* New York: Vintage Books, 1964. 370 pages.
(A comprehensive overview of the interracial situation in the United States.)

Simpson, George E. and John M. Yinger. *Racial and Cultural Minorities,* third edition. New York: Harper and Row, 1965. 582 pages.
(Analysis of patterns of prejudice and discrimination.)

"The Negro In America: What Must Be Done," *Newsweek,* November 20, 1967.
(Self-explanatory)

Taba, Hilda, Elizabeth Hall Brady and John T. Robinson. *Intergroup Education in Public Schools.* Washington: American Council on Education, 1952. 337 pages.
(Program patterns developed by a number of schools engaged in the Project in Intergroup Education.)

Treager, Helen and Marian Radke Yarrow. *They Learn What They Live; Prejudice in Young Children.* New York: Harper and Brothers, 1952. 392 pages.
(Origins and development of prejudice in first- and second-graders.)

Van Til, William. "Civil Rights and Humanization," *Humanizing Education,* The Association for Supervision and Curriculum Development, 1967, pages 89–103.
(A brief re-cap of the struggle for civil rights and the suggestion that the goal of this age must be human rights.)

Weinberg, Meyer, ed. *School Integration: A comprehensive classified bibliography of 3,100 references.* Chicago: Integrated Education Associates, 1967. 137 pages.

Intergroup Education Pamphlets published by the National Conference of Christians and Jews, 381 Fourth Avenue, New York, New York 10016. Some titles:

Beauchamp, Mary, Ardelle Llewellyn and Vivienne S. Worley. *Building Brotherhood: What Can Elementary Schools Do?*

Bostwick, Prudence. *Brotherhood: What Can Secondary Schools Do?*

Heaton, Margaret M. *Feelings Are Facts.*

Shaftel, George and Fannie R. *Role Playing the Problem Story.*

Pamphlets of the Institute of Human Relations Press, The American Jewish Committee, 165 East 56th Street, New York, New York 10022. Some titles:

Edwards, George. *The Police on the Urban Frontier.*

Miel, Alice with Edwin Kiester, Jr. *The Short Changed Children of Suburbia.*

Wolfgang, Marvin E. *Crime and Race: Conceptions and Misconceptions.*

Integrated Education, published bi-monthly by Integrated Education Associates, 33 South Dearborn Street, Chicago, Illinois 60604. (Current problems and progress in integration and quality education.)

Index

Achievement:

desegregation effects on, 127–131
and the sense of control of the
environment, 126

Appalachian migrants, 68–69, 70

Armor, David J., 128

Association patterns, 96–98

Attitudes:

awareness of, 42–46
and words, 175–176

Authority, attitudes toward, 141–
142

Baldwin, James, 194

Behavior:

crowd, 136–137
developmental levels of, 118 119
irrational, 136–137
in multi-group schools, 95–96
rationalization, 145–146
self-awareness of, 42–46
unconscious motivation in, 144–
145

Blake, William, 188

Bontemps, Arna, 192, 194

Brownell, William A., 178

Bussing, 29, 32–33, 37–38

Buswell, Guy T., 178

Catholics, 71

Clark, Kenneth B., 129

Coleman, Clice C., 188

Coleman, James S., 126–129

Conflict incidents.

analyzing, 98–99
and discussion, 43–45
(*See also* Hostility)

Communication:

across group lines, 33–35
lack of, 90
teacher-student, 34–35
and vocabulary, 87–88

Crime and intergroup relations,
156–157

Crowd behavior, 136–137

"Cultural deprivation," 73

Curriculum:

integrating areas of knowledge,
179–180
for minority children, 85–86

Desegregation: 32–33

and communication, 33–35
and conflict, 38 39
effects on achievement, 127–131

Discipline:

and emotional expression, 117–
118
and intergroup relations, 121–
122
and noise, 116–117
problems, as internal disharmony, 112–115
and self-control, 119–121

Emotional expression, 117–118

Environment:

in multi-group schools, 84–85
sense of control of, 126

Epithets, use of, 24–25, 44, 51

Fear, effect on judgment, 137–138

Fights, *see* Conflict incidents

Frost, Frances, 192

Gangs, 71–72

Gordon, Sol, 129

Grouping:
  ability, 112
  homogeneous, 111–112

Guilt:
  effect on judgment, 137–138
  national, 147

Hansen, C. F., 131

Hostility: 42
  and fear, 143–144; *see also* Fear
  and guilt, 146–147; *see also* Guilt
  and inner conflict, 142–143
  (*See also* Conflict incidents)

Hughes, Langston, 189, 192

Hunger, 167–169

Integration:
  defined, 40–41
  dynamic, 44–45, 46
  needs and methods, 41–46
  social class, 72–74

Interdependence of man, 1

Intergroup relations:
  classroom discussions on, 43–45, 91–95
  dichotomous thinking in, 5, 139–140
  and discipline, 121–122
  and educational practices, 29–31
  evaluation checklist, 100–105
  first grade unit in, 199–204
  and homogeneous grouping, 111–112
  in-service programs in, 110
  teaching, 23–27, 109–111, 115, 122, 148–151, 197
  and traditional intercultural units, 46
  universal needs in, 74–75

Jewett, Arno, 135

Johnson, Grace Nail, 191

Johnson, James Weldon, 189–191

Judgment, effect of fear and guilt on, 137–138

Klineberg, Otto, 131

Kokeritz, Helge, 135

Kottmeyer, William, 173

Language and intergroup relations, 176–177

Legal rights of minorities, 157–159

Lesser, Gerald S., 131

Lower-class children, desirable characteristics, 73–74

Majority children:
  delusion of no prejudice, 61–62
  isolation of, 57–59
  stereotyping behavior, 59–61
  unrealistic self-image, 26–27

McAulay, J. D., 116

Migratory farm workers, 70

Minority children:
  control of the environment, 126
  creativity of, 88–89
  honesty in, 88
  inner conflict, 26
  isolation, 10
  overcompensation, 65
  school achievement, 127–131
  school environment, 84–85
  self-concept, 123–126
  self-rejection, 4
  transferred, 130; *see also* Bussing
  vocabularies of, 87–88
  white, problems of, 64–66
  white values, 83–84, 99

Myrdal, Gunnar, 147

National Conference of Christians and Jews, 110

Negro History week, 113–114, 124

Negro prose and poetry, 189–194

Otto, James H., 182

Parker, Alfred E., 191

Pennsylvania Dutch, 155

Peterson, Miriam E., 191

Police-minority group relations, 141–142

Poor whites, 71–72, 74–75

Poverty:
cycle of, 75
and food, 167

Prejudice:
in children, 2
intra-group, 67–69
and lack of knowledge, 138–139
mathematical analogy, 180–181
and non-participation, 66–67
universality of, 164

Press, freedom and responsibility of, 156–157

Prouty, Charles T., 135

Pupil interest and involvement, 119–121

Readers, elementary, 194–196

Reissman, Frank, 89, 127

Religion:
freedom of, 153–156
in the public schools, 81, 154

Revolution and rioting, 165–166

Robinson, Helen M., 195

Role-playing, 107–109

Sauble, Irene, 178

Schneider, Herman and Nina, 167

Schools, multi-group:
curriculum factors, 85–86; see also Curriculum
environment in, 84–85
evaluation checklist, 100–105
internal disharmony in, 112–115
patterns of association, 96–98
recognizing feelings in, 99–100
suburban, 77–78

Science and cooperation, 171–172

Segregation:
causes of, 27–29
harmful effects of, 23–25

Self-awareness in the classroom, 42–46

Self-concept, minority child, 123–126

Self-hate, group, 146

Self-worth, sense of, 113–114

Slavery in America, 160–163, 190

Social change, 148

Social class integration, 72–74

Stereotyping, 12, 59–61

Suburbs:
middle-class, 78–80
minorities in, 80–82
working-class, 76–78

Teacher:
analyzing the fights, 98–99
encouraging discussion, 93–95
evaluation checklist, 100–105
intergroup skills, 50–53
observing behavior, 95–96
raising issues, 91–93
recognizing feelings, 99–100
sociometric techniques, 96–98
suppression, 20
taking the initiative, 106–107

Teacher Corps, 110

Teaching, cooperative, 109–111

Theobald, John R., 188

Tokenism, 35–37

Towle, Albert, 182

Urban League, 110

Vote, right to, 158

Wade, Louise C., 152

Wade, Richard C., 152

War and human relations, 163–164

Ware, Kay, 173

WASPs, minority-group, 70–71

White power, 62–63

White values of minority children, 83–84

Wilder, Howard B., 152

Wilson, Alan B., 128

Witty, Paul, 191

Wolman, T. G., 130

Words:
   and attitudes, 175–176
   and meanings, 173–175

Wright, Mrs. Ellen, 194

Wright, Richard, 194

Zenger, John Peter, 156